Passport to Web Radio

Music, sports, news and entertainment from the hometowns of your world.

ISSN 1091-840X

OUR READER IS THE MOST IMPORTANT PERSON IN THE WORLD!

Editorial

Editor-in-Chief	Lawrence Magne
Editor	David Walcutt
Contributing Editors	Tony Jones
	John Campbell
Graphic Arts	Bad Cat Design, cover; Mike Wright, text
Artwork	Gahan Wilson, cover
Printing	World Color Press

Administration

Publisher	Lawrence Magne
Associate Publisher	Jane Brinker
Distribution	Mary Kroszner, MWK
Offices	IBS North America, Box 300, Penn's Park PA 18943, USA; www.passport.com
	Distribution: Phone +1 (215) 794-3410; Fax +1 (215) 794 3396; mwk@passport.com
	Editorial: Fax +1 (215) 598 3794
	Orders (24 hours): Phone +1 (215) 794-8252; Fax +1 (215) 794 3396; mwk@passport.com; www.passport.com
Media Communications	Jock Elliott, Pickering Lane, Troy NY 12180, USA; Fax +1 (518) 271 6131; media@passport.com

IBS Bureaus

IBS Latin America	Tony Jones, Casilla 1844, Asunción, Paraguay; Fax +595 (21) 420 010; schedules@passport.com
IBS Australia	Craig Tyson, Box 2145, Malaga WA 6062; Fax +61 (8) 9342 9158; addresses@passport.com
IBS Japan	Toshimichi Ohtake, 5-31-6 Tamanawa, Kamakura 247; Fax +81 (467) 43 2167; ibsjapan@passport.com

PASSPORT, PASSPORT TO WORLD BAND RADIO, *WorldScan*, *Radio Database International*, *RDI White Papers* and *White Papers* are registered trademarks of International Broadcasting Services, Ltd., in the United States, Canada, United Kingdom and various other parts of the world.

Copyright © 1998 International Broadcasting Services, Ltd.
All rights reserved. No part of this publication may be reproduced, stored in a retrieval system, or transmitted in any form or by any means without the prior written consent of the publisher.

Passport to Web Radio
Second Edition

TABLE OF CONTENTS

Foreplay

4 Compleat Idiot's Guide to Getting Started
Eight pages, then catch the world.

12 When Is Teatime in Tahiti?
Local time anywhere in the world.

What's On

16 Prime Cuts
Alternative from Adelaide, Zarathustra from Zagreb.

30 NetRadio: How Music Should Be (Almost)
Cool concept poorly executed, or just a bad idea?

40 Voices from Home
Fasten your seat belts—1,550 stations from Andorra to Yugoslavia.

Around the Bend

124 Web Radio's Unexpected Future
It's not what Microsoft plans, says John Campbell.

132 Webcasting: Can It Pay?
Kim Komando's formula for success.

136 Is Traditional Radio Doomed?
Webcasting's wireless future looms large.

142 The Slippery Slope of Piglet Radio
Is pioneer KPIG pointing the way, or screwing up?

Compleat Idiot's Guide to Getting Started

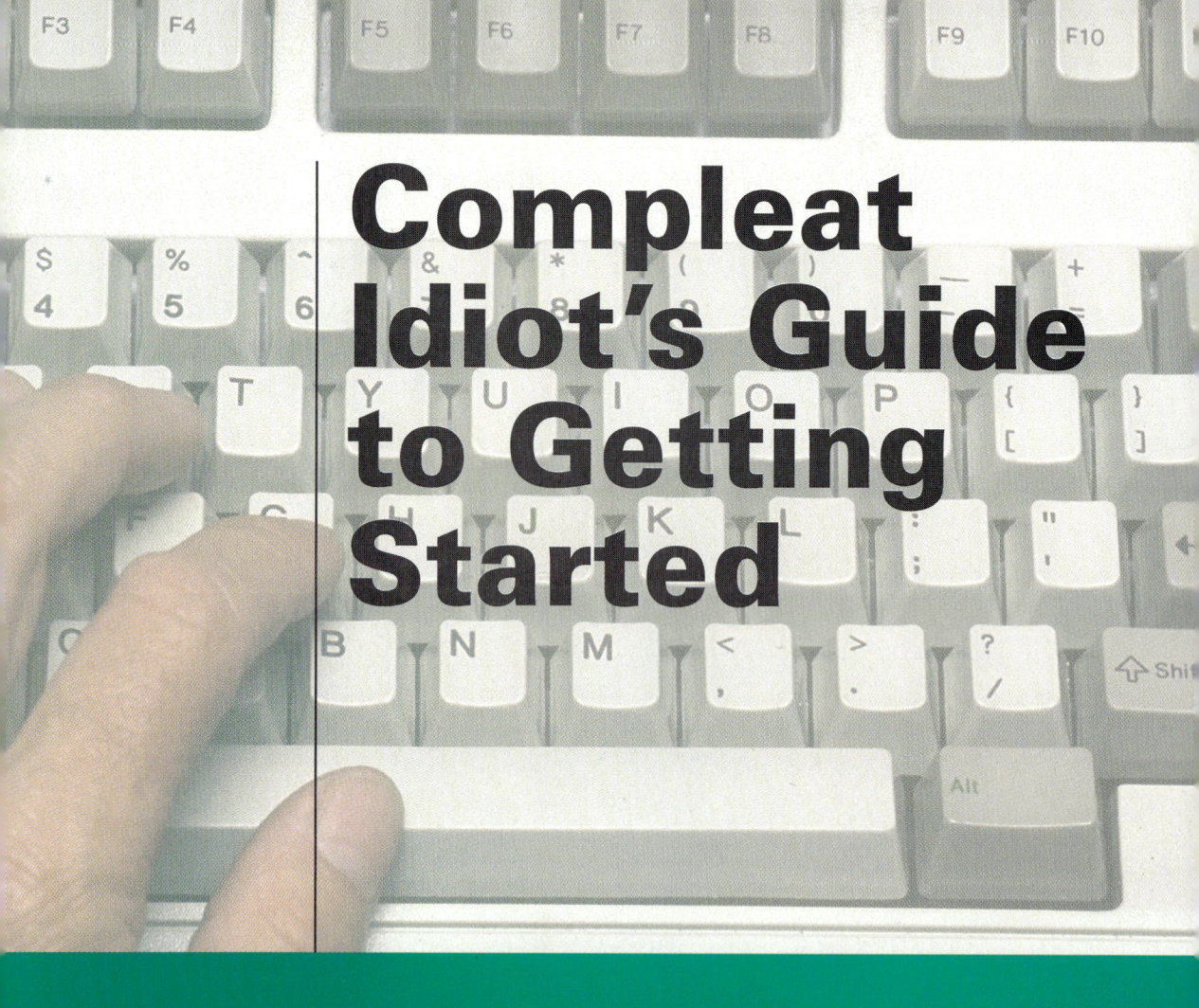

Over 1,550 channels, and look where it's headed!

In August 1996, there were 178 stations from 32 countries. By December 1996, there were 390 stations from 50 nations. By mid-1998, this had increased to over 1,550 stations in 101 countries.

Some are in native tongues, but the majority are in English. Most are pre-existing AM, FM and similar broadcasters or networks that simulcast on the Web.

Programs Live or When You Want Them

Most Web radio stations are aired live, but some are only on-demand. Stations with on-demand programs have a library of prerecorded shows that you can hear whenever you wish—like a video store, except it's audio instead of video, and you don't have to drive anywhere or pay anything. The best stations offer both live programming and on-demand archives, letting you choose whichever you prefer.

Listen While You Work . . . or Play

With Windows 98/95/NT and other operating systems that allow for multitasking, you can keep working at your computer the way you normally do, but at the same time listen to Zydeco from New Orleans, or tamboritzas from Zagreb. You can even browse the Internet while listening to radio on the Web.

Whether Web radio will cost you anything depends on the specifics of your setup. If your computer is already online and appropriately configured—new ones are usually ready to rock 'n' roll—the cost should be nil. See "What You'll Need," below, to find out the score.

RealAudio—Web Radio's Current Standard

Nearly every Web radio station now uses RealAudio, RealNetworks' software package for real time "streamed" audio through the Internet. Stations that don't use RealAudio may use StreamWorks, pioneering streaming software which, although free, is relatively "hiccupy" at 28.8k. That and Microsoft's NetShow—interestingly, RealNetworks is 20 percent owned by Microsoft—may seriously challenge RealAudio as DSL and other broadband modems become increasingly commonplace (see below).

RealAudio originally operated at 14.4k, and like many new computer applications tended to disappoint once the novelty wore thin. Even ordinary talk could be difficult to understand, and music was hopeless.

But now it's operating primarily at 28.8k and up, the rates used by today's modems. Combined with ever-better versions of RealAudio, 28.8 connections have brought Web radio to the point where most folks can now hear stations that sound better than local AM stations—much better, as stations like California's experienced KPIG shows (KPIG was the world's first commercial Web radio station).

Johan Pretorius handles the early morning shift at Radio Hoogland, part of the South African Stud Book and Livestock Improvement Association in Bloemfontein, South Africa. Their slogan: "The blue-blooded people."

Studbook

But there are catches. One is that stations pay for RealAudio upgrades, so some save money by using old software that produces excessive "static" and echos. Another is that the result is no better than the weakest link in the communications chain. No matter how fast your modem, if the Internet is busy reception will degrade as the percentage of packet re-sends increases.

Additionally, in some countries the Internet is more like a straw than a pipeline, producing prime-time audio that would have made Marconi wince. And even when the Webcasting software is recent and the Internet in good shape, a station's or network's server may be tied up, leaving you unable to make a connection. (Fortunately, "sharing" arrangements such as IP multicasting and networks like broadcast.com help keep this problem at bay.)

With 56k modems and a quiet Internet, Web radio can sound virtually like local FM-stereo—yet, evolving alternatives are even better. For example, there's DSL (digital subscriber line, also ADSL Lite and Universal ADSL). DSL modems allow for CD quality even at 256k settings. Telcos plan to equip most of North America with 256 kbps–1.5 Mbps—possibly eventually up to 8 Mbps—in 1999 and 2000, with monthly fees starting not far above current 28.8/33.6/56k charges.

When New Zealand's Mark Nicholls isn't using his PC to hear Web radio, he turns to Passport to World Band Radio and his Sony shortwave to enjoy everything from New Guinea tribal stations to Israel Radio.
T. Ohtake

Echo of Moscow brings NewsTalk radio to Russians worldwide.
Echo of Moscow

Two-way cable modems already have downstream throughputs of 1–10 Mbps, and are not terribly costly if you already have a cable TV hookup. However, cable-modem service is only being made available slowly.

Looking upward, DirecPC's satellite network can downlink at up to 400 kbps, although it's usually less. Notwithstanding its cost as a standalone service, it is relatively affordable when obtained as a package along with DirecTV. Turn-of-the-century satellite networks such as Iridium and Celestri should downlink at up to 64 Mbps . . . if you've got deep pockets.

Looking ahead, by 2003 broadband wireless technologies (local multipoint distribution system, LMDS) and fiber-optic cables should be available to provide up to 50–100 Mbps throughput in many locations.

RealAudio's other high cards are simplicity and reliability. Once you get to a station's Web site, all you do is click on the RealAudio or other obvious icon or link. In seconds, if the station's audio server is available and operating properly, the station is booming away and stays locked in. With most browsers, a handy volume slider appears on your screen, too, and with Windows can be brought back up at any time just by clicking the RealAudio button on the taskbar at the bottom of the screen.

You can get RealAudio in a free version or a fancy version, but at 28.8 the free one sounds only a skootch less good than the $30 fancy offering, and above 28.8 there's no audible difference. Also, you have to pay $20 a year for upgrades to the $30 version, whereas upgrades to the free version are gratis. So unless you're big on channel hopping, save your money and go with the freebie.

Although Bose and others make computer speakers that cost several hundred dollars, Boston Acoustics' MicroMedia is a real winner at under $200.

iQ 3D Audio

A better deal offered by RealNetworks and others is iQ 3D Audio from QSound Labs, which loads automatically at each bootup. Like the expansion sound you get on new TVs and VCRs, or Dolby at the movies, it juices up the audio to give it a wider, more expansive sound. It helps, but it's like getting loans—when you need iQ most, like with a 28.8 mono signal, it does the least. But give it an already great-sounding 56k stereo signal, and the improvement is even greater.

As of presstime, iQ is $20 from www.realstore.com/realstore/order.iq_hp.html, or $25 from the Alberta manufacturer at www.qsound.ca/cprod0.htm. Either way, even for 28.8 signals, for music lovers it is worth considering.

What You Need

• **Computer.** You've heard it all before, "Your PC should have a 486 processor or better, at least 8 Mb of RAM and Windows 3.1.x, blah, blah." And you also know that in the real world the minimum you really need is a 90 MHz or better Pentium processor, 16 Mb or more of memory and Windows 98/95 for an operating system. Web radio is no different, although you can get your feet wet using older legacy hardware. Non-Wintel users note: Macs with PowerPC or 680x0 processors and an OS 7.x operating system are also fully supported, as is IBM OS/2.

COMPLEAT IDIOT'S GUIDE TO GETTING STARTED

- **Audio Board.** Another "must" is a good audio board, along with suitable drivers/software—today's home computers usually come with these already installed. If you use a PC, as opposed to a Mac, be sure the board is Sound Blaster compatible and 16-bit.

- **Speakers.** Amplified and shielded computer speakers or headphones last a very long time, and Web audio quality is improving dramatically. If your system's existing speakers are mediocre, or it doesn't have any, forget Chinese cheapies and get an affordable three-piece system that will stroke your ears, like the Cambridge SoundWorks ($150, www.hifi.com/soundwks.html), Boston Acoustics Micro-Media ($200, www.bostonacoustics.com) or Boston Acoustics MediaTheater ($300)—each of these is among the best in its price class.

- **Modem.** Your modem should operate at 28.8 or above. A 14.4 modem will allow you to receive a fading roster of lo-fi offerings, but don't say you weren't warned. Right now, 56k modems aren't the advantage they should be, but this is changing fast as stations and telcos upgrade. Even at around 40k actual throughput, the improvement over that of a 28.8 modem is just enough to allow Web radio to really shine. If you want earthquake sound and blazing fidelity, check out DSL when it comes to your area—basic 256k service is more than adequate—or two-way cable. If wired Internet connections are not satisfactory at your location, consider a satellite network, choosing carefully among the various price plans.

- **Internet Service Provider.** Almost any ISP handles Web radio properly via 14.4/28.8/33.6/56 modems or ISDN, but with

Kim Komando's radio shows attract a huge following, but that's only part of it. Her Website—www.komando.com—is packed with common-sense advice for those trying to live harmoniously with cantankerous PCs. (And, yes, that's her real name.)

Komando Corporation

The Kim Komando Computer Minute

Panama's Radio Mia serves up news, commentary, sports and musical variety—all in *español*.
R. D. y C., S.A.

higher-speed options be prepared to be locked into the company providing the tie-in. If you're on AOL or CompuServe, see whether Web radio comes through satisfactorily; if not, contact them for the most recent software or try another ISP. Remember, results depend not only on your ISP, but also the local phone circuits. In North America and much of Europe, most will handle 20–50k throughput, but in some other places even 14.4 is chancy.

☞ If you're going to be listening to Web radio for hours on end and aren't using DSL or two-way cable, having a flat-fee phone-line rate for unlimited calling between your computer and the ISP may be cheaper than a per-minute arrangement. Call your local phone provider(s) for specific options.

☞ Although ISPs usually disconnect if you are inactive for 20 minutes or so, the incoming Web radio signal qualifies as "use." So as long as you're listening, the ISP connection to the Web will stay open—a more ethical and pleasant means than "pinging" for keeping your circuit open, provided your PC has sufficient resources to handle this degree of multitasking without slowing down excessively. (Also, see the second ☞ icon under "Web Browser," below.)

• **Web Browser.** Microsoft Internet Explorer v3.0 and above and Netscape Navigator v3.0 and above both work great with Web radio, and they're free.

☞ If you are still using Windows 95 and eventually have to reload it for some reason, you'll also have to reload the latest RealAudio and your preferred version of Internet Explorer, as Windows 95 contains ancient versions of these that may overwrite the new versions you had loaded up earlier.

☞ Your browser may automatically disconnect from the Web if you don't tickle the ivories every so often. This can be a nuisance if you're trying to listen without interruption, so set your browser so it won't disconnect. For example, with Internet Explorer click on View, Options, Connection, then click off the arrow for "Disconnect if idle for . . . ," then click OK.

• **Streaming Software.** Even if your browser comes with RealAudio, you'll want to download the latest version. The current RealAudio can be downloaded for free from Web radio sites, or by going to www.real.com/products/player/index.html. For StreamWorks download, go to www.xingtech.com/downloads/sw, while NetShow's download page is www.microsoft.com/netshow/download.htm.

• **Web Anti-Virus Software.** Need we restate the obvious? Downloading files from the Internet can introduce catastrophic viruses into your computer, so solid A-V software, such as Norton Anti-Virus or Norton Utilities (evaluation versions from www.symantec.com/trialware/index.html or purchase from http://shop.symantec.com) is a "must." Get this loaded up first and don't forget to download upgrades periodically.

☞ IBM's Watson Research skunk works is about to release an upgraded A-V "Immune System for Cyberspace" (www.research.ibm.com/topics/smart/security), which has the ability to automatically create a cure when a new virus is first encountered.

• **Zip/unzip software** to download audio material on file. Downloadable automatically for free, when needed, from various Web radio sites, or you can download an evaluation version of WinZip from www.winzip.com/download.cgi.

That's it, soup-to-nuts! Once you're up and running, turn the page and check out the hundreds of hometown and worldwide stations waiting to be enjoyed.

_____

Prepared by Lawrence Magne, with Tony Jones.

Denis Fortin prepares to interview France Damour for his show over CKOI, Verdun, Quebec.
CKOI

When Is Teatime in Tahiti?

What happens if you want to know the time in the country you're listening to? After all, the station you're trying to hear in Kumquat, Mongolia might not be responding because it's 3:00 AM in that part of the world. Or maybe you want to hear the Six O'clock Evening News, but need to know the time at your location which corresponds to 6:00 PM over there.

Midyear Madness
Sounds simple, but while it may be Daylight Saving or Summer Time in your part of the world, the country you're trying to hear may keep the same time all year round. This can screw up the midyear time differential. And if the station is in the Southern Hemisphere, its time change may be the reverse of what happens in the Northern Hemisphere. A double whammy.

Trying to do it "my place against your place" can get so confusing that even the pros may get it wrong. One Asian station which also uses Web radio has been known to announce not only the local time, but also the time in Washington, D.C. However, some months of the year its Washington announcements are off by an hour. To make matters worse, the time check is sponsored by one of the world's leading manufacturers of clocks and watches!

One Time for One World

The fix is easy: World Time, invented long ago in Greenwich, England so mariners would know the time no matter where they were. PASSPORT lets you determine local time in another country by adding or subtracting from World Time, also known as Coordinated Universal Time (UTC, the modern designation), Greenwich Mean Time (GMT, the traditional term) or Zulu (military lingo).

First, you need to set a clock to World Time. To do this, go to tycho.usno.navy.mil/what.html. This U.S. Navy site—those seafarers, again!—tells you not only World Time, but also local times throughout North America. A chart showing the differences between World Time and the various American local times is at tycho.usno.navy.mil/zones.html. World Time is also available, albeit unofficially, at the simpler URL of www.wclv.com/audio.

Display Time on Screen or Separate Clock

World Time doesn't change seasonally. Too, it uses a 24-hour, rather than a 12-hour, clock, so 2:00 PM comes out as 14:00. Once you use World Time, you'll see why this 24-hour format is a godsend.

The simplest way to show World Time would be to change your computer's clock and have it display on the screen. Alas, operating systems often don't allow for time in 24-hour format.

However, cheap 24-hour desk clocks work well. Try the $9.95 MFJ-24-207B (www.mfjenterprises.com) or the $14.95 walnut-framed NI8F LCD (www.universal-radio.com). Thumbs down, though, on those fancy "World Time" clocks on jeweler's shelves. Extra money aside, the by-country time information they give is sometimes off by one or even two hours.

Once you've got a clock showing World Time, you can use this listing to determine the hour wherever there is a Web radio station.

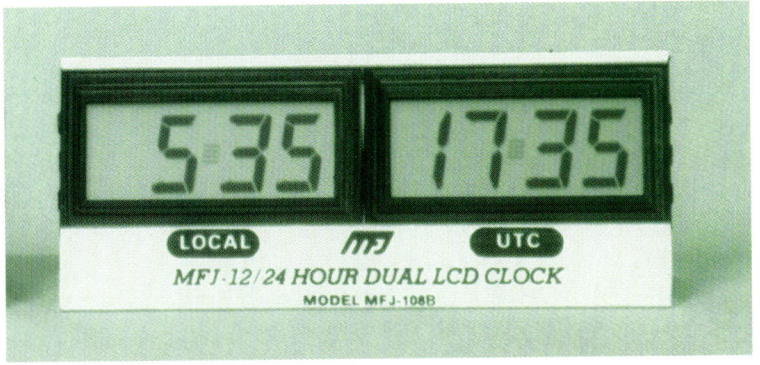

MFJ's affordable dual-zone timepiece stands out because it gives local time in the customary 12-hour AM/PM, whereas it shows World Time in a 24-hour format. MFJ is at www.mfjenterprises.com.

HOW TO DETERMINE LOCAL TIME

Station Location — *Local Time*

North America

Newfoundland St. John's NF, St. Anthony NF	World Time −3½ hours winter, −2½ hours summer
Atlantic St. John NB, Battle Harbour NF	World Time −4 hours winter, −3 hours summer
Eastern New York, Atlanta, Toronto	World Time −5 hours winter, −4 hours summer
Central Chicago, Winnipeg, Mexico City	World Time −6 hours winter, −5 hours summer
Mountain Denver, Calgary, Hermosillo	World Time −7 hours winter, −6 hours summer
Pacific San Francisco, Vancouver, Mexicali	World Time −8 hours winter, −7 hours summer
Alaska Anchorage, Fairbanks	World Time −9 hours winter, −8 hours summer

Caribbean, Central & South America

Brazil (Eastern)	World Time −2 hours local summer, −3 hours local winter (midyear); (northeastern Brazil −3 hours year round)
Argentina, Suriname, Uruguay	World Time −3 hours
Brazil (Western), Chile, Paraguay	World Time −3 hours local summer, −4 hours local winter (midyear); (northwestern Brazil −4 hours year round)
Eastern Caribbean (West Indies) Barbados, Dominican Republic, French & Netherlands Antilles, Virgin Islands	World Time −4 hours
Bolivia, Venezuela	World Time −4 hours
Brazil (Acre)	World Time −5 hours
Colombia, Ecuador, Panama, Peru	World Time −5 hours
Western Caribbean Bahamas, Haiti	World Time −5 hours winter (−4 hours summer)
Central America (exc. Panama)	World Time −6 hours

Europe

Iceland	World Time exactly
Ireland, Portugal, United Kingdom	World Time winter, World Time +1 hour summer

Continental Western Europe; parts of Central and Eastern Continental Europe Berlin, Stockholm, Prague	World Time +1 hour winter, +2 hours summer
Elsewhere in Continental Europe Belarus, Bulgaria, Cyprus, Estonia, Finland, Greece, Latvia, Lithuania, Moldova, Romania, Russia (Kaliningradskaya Oblast), Turkey, Ukraine	World Time +2 hours winter, +3 hours summer

Africa & Mideast

Ghana, Morocco, Senegal	World Time exactly
Tunisia	World Time +1 hour
South Africa, Zambia, Zimbabwe	World Time +2 hours
Egypt, Israel, Jordan, Lebanon, West Bank/Gaza	World Time +2 hours winter, +3 hours summer
Kenya, Kuwait	World Time +3 hours
Oman, Reunion	World Time +4 hours

West & South Asia

Iran	World Time +3½ hours winter, +4½ hours summer
Pakistan	World Time +5 hours
India	World Time +5 1/2 hours
Nepal	World Time +5 3/4 hours
Bangladesh, Sri Lanka	World Time +6 hours

East and Southeast Asia, Australasia and Pacific

Thailand, Indonesia (Bandung, Jakarta, Medan)	World Time +7 hours
China, including Hong Kong and Taiwan; Malaysia; Philippines; Singapore	World Time +8 hours
Japan, Korea	World Time +9 hours
Australia (Victoria, New South Wales, Tasmania)	World Time +11 hours Australian summer, +10 Australian winter (midyear)
Australia (South Australia)	World Time +10½ hours Australian summer, +9½ hours Australian winter (midyear)
Australia (Queensland)	World Time +10 hours
Australia (Northern Territory)	World Time +9½ hours
Australia (Western Australia)	World Time +8 hours
Guam, Papua New Guinea	World Time +10 hours
New Zealand	World Time +13 hours New Zealand summer, +12 hours New Zealand winter (midyear)
French Polynesia and Hawai'i	World Time −10 hours

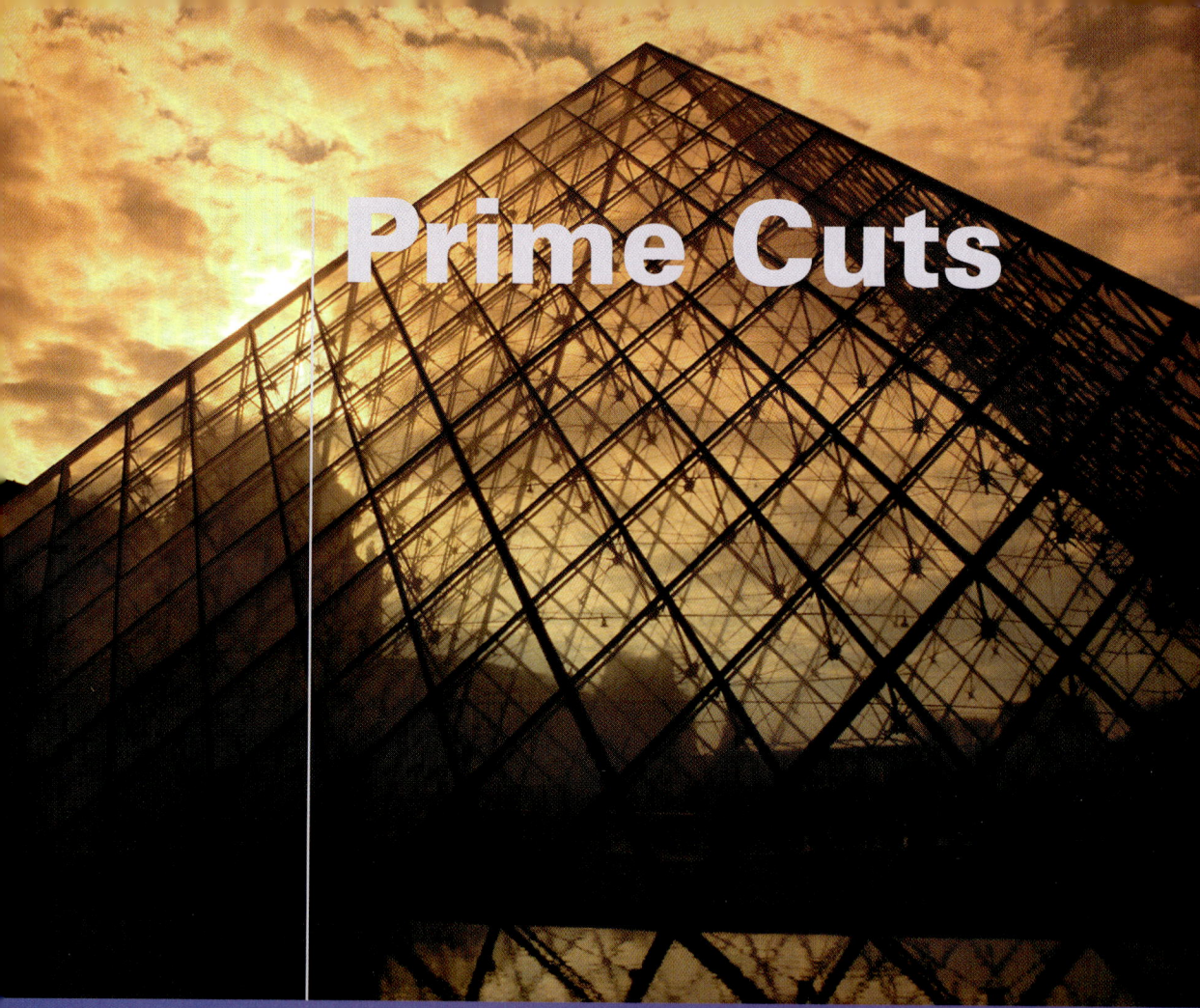

Prime Cuts

There are over 1,550 stations on the Web, as detailed in PASSPORT's "Voices from Home" section. Most are predictable—interesting mainly for their local news, sports and weather—but some push the envelope of entertainment and information beyond the ordinary.

These are the stations we feel are the best on the cyberwaves. However, to some extent unusual offerings tend to be less technically reliable than others, so be patient, especially during times of 'Net congestion. This tends to be worst between 5:00–8:00 PM Eastern Time in North America, plus Americans listening to stations abroad may also encounter 'Net congestion local evenings at the station end (see "When Is Teatime in Tahiti?").

If you encounter breaks or connection difficulties, try again at a less popular hour.

☞ All stations are in RealAudio unless otherwise indicated.

☞ If you can't find where to click for audio, look for ".ram" appearing in your browser's status bar.

☞ Sometimes you can't connect because a station's Web address (URL) has been altered. To get around this, try shortening the URL by a segment or two between slashes. For example, if www.axolotl.edu/WPOO fails, try www.axolotl.edu, then follow the on-screen links to the station's new audio page.

African

American, African and Caribbean musical styles are so intertwined that it is tempting to bunch them all together. But the reality is more complex and synergistic, especially when the language is not English. Some of the better examples . . .

Metro FM, Johannesburg, South Africa, www.qradio.net. Mix of American urban and Soweto hip-hop.

Radio Nostalgie Dakar, Senegal, www.metissacana.sn/nostalgie. West African pop, largely in French, but the server is frustratingly balky. Senegal generates some of the most interesting music on the African continent.

Big Band/Crooners

This is the great music of the period that started with the Depression, then faded away with the prosperity that followed the Korean War. It is usually thought of as the music of the GI generation, but it is finally being recognized for what it is: not just music of a certain time, but a distinct and worthy American genre that, like jazz, has become part of the permanent musical repertoire.

NetRadio, Minneapolis, Minnesota, www.netradio.net/jazz (click on Big Band or Classic Crooners). Miller, Goodman, Crosby, Cole and "Bones" are all here, with nary an ad. Tune in, hep cats and gals in radioland!

☞ *Catch:* Your PC may wind up downloading NetRadio's on-screen ads, which on slower machines chews up so many

Cécile Sow of Radio Nostalgie Dakar, Senegal, is responsible for "Zapping," a French-language cultural report aired each Monday, Wednesday and Friday at 10:45 World Time. Nostalgie

resources that the music hiccups. *Solution:* Get RealAudio working, then exit the browser.

WJUX, Monticello, New York, www.radio.broadcast.com/radio/Classics/WJUX. There are precious few stations, public or commercial, still gracing the airwaves with big band dance music from the thirties, forties and fifties. WJUX, fighting for its legal status as an FM broadcaster, is looking in part to the Web for its future. Assuming the station hangs in there—as of presstime, broadcast.com was "temporarily" not airing it—this station is "must" listening if you are an enthusiast of the big band era.

WRCT, Pittsburgh, Pennsylvania, www.wrct.org. "The Big Bang" airs big band, swing and jazz in the wee hours of Sunday morning (or late Saturday night, if you prefer) from 1 to 3 AM Eastern Time. Audioactive and Shockwave only, though.

Brazilian

Rádio Musical, São Paulo, Brazil, www.uol.com.br/musical. One of Brazil's best spots for *Música Popular Brasileira (MPB)*. Don't be fooled by "popular"—in Brazil, that's not the usual all-embracing term, but rather a modern musical genre in its own right.

Rádio Tropical, Rio de Janeiro, Brazil, tropical.hipernet.com.br. A nice on-demand sampling of various types of traditional, *Carnaval* and modern Brazilian music, as well as live Brazilian news, music and *futebol*. Some technical glitches.

Classical

Classical music tends to be embraced by those who identify with an ordered, formal society of team players—hardly the society of *fin de siecle grungé*, and it shows. Over the past ten years the average age of classical music listeners in the United States has slipped from 45 to 55, and classical music has all but vanished from the airwaves in the U.S. and much of Europe.

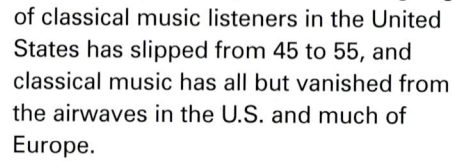

In order to reverse this trend, classical stations are increasingly embracing "popular classical" formats, where few full symphonies are played and challenging pieces are left off playlists. The rationale is that classical music should reach the widest number of people possible, certainly a more satisfactory conclusion than Beethoven de-composing.

*Even youngsters get into the swing of things during Brazil's **Carnaval** festivities.*
Rádio Liberdade

Yet, the rich offerings of the Internet allow for more serious fare, as well. Indeed, there is no other vehicle for the classical music lover that even remotely equals Web radio. With greater offerings and wider bandwidths in the offing, Web radio could be the salvation of this important genre.

Two flies in the ointment: First, classical, more than any other type of music, suffers from rights restrictions. Thus, many syndicated orchestras and opera houses require most stations not to air their programs over the Web. Presumably this will be sorted out over time. Second, audience bets are sometimes hedged by offering classical/jazz, etc. formats, just as non-Web station WRTI in Philadelphia has been doing since all-classical WFLN, then on the Web via broadcast.com, was replaced by rocker WXXM in 1998.

Full-time Classical

Accent 4, Strasbourg, France, www.cybercable.tm.fr/~yklaiber/accueil_fr.htm. Worthy listening around-the-clock with no ads . . . but it requires at least a 33.6k connection, with a 56k modem being a safer bet outside the European Community. This station appears to be primarily a sales tool for a high-bandwidth French/E.C. Internet service provider, which presumably accounts for its not being receivable on lower-bandwidth modems.

Classic FM, London, United Kingdom, www.classicfm.co.uk. Music that is pleasant, rather than challenging. A popular commercial format, aired night and day by Virgin on FM outlets throughout the U.K.

HRT3, Croatia, www.hrt.hr/streams/streams_eng.html (click on "HR3"). Great classical music, including opera, from Zagreb, Croatia—a capital in the war-ravaged Balkans, and one of the last places you might expect to find exemplary cultural broadcasts using advanced technology. If you can't connect, remember that they are off the air weeknights during their local early morning, which takes place several hours ahead of American time zones. No commentary in English, but it still gets high marks from PASSPORT's fussy panelists.

KBYU, Provo, Utah. Brigham Young University's 24-hour public radio station airs a wide variety of symphonic and chamber music, in addition to opera excerpts, classical guitar, choral music and early music. There's also MPR's excellent "St. Paul Sunday," and at various times of the week Latter-day Saints' devotionals and other inspirational programming are interspersed.

KING, Seattle, www.king.org/content/real_audio_area/index.html. This is the granddaddy of Web radio classical music stations, and it shows. Fine musical offerings, sans ads, plus they are ahead of the curve in handling "rights blackouts" with grace.

KLASI, Dallas, Texas, www.broadcast.com/radio/internal/asx/klasi. The in-house classical outlet of Web radio network broadcast.com. Uses NetShow.

KRTS, Houston, Texas, www.radio.broadcast.com/radio/Classical/KRTS. Around-the-clock playlist of over 2,000 pieces are aired over this commercial fine arts station. Among its high points are weekly broadcasts from the outstanding Houston Grand Opera and the Houston Symphony, as well as the Houston Ballet.

NetRadio Classical, Minneapolis, www.netradio.net/classical. Think of this as an on-ground airline audio system, but with all your channel choices being classical—baroque, chants, operas, symphonies and so on. It's a great idea, especially as you hear no ads.

☞ *Catch:* Your PC may wind up downloading NetRadio's on-screen ads, which on slower machines chews up so many resources that the music hiccups. *Solution:* Get RealAudio working, then exit the browser.

Radio Beethoven, Santiago, Chile, www.beethovenfm.cl/RealAudio/index.html. Chile is the great success story of South America, and not only in its economy. Its love of fine culture goes back generations, and is exquisitely exemplified by Radio Beethoven, one of the classical treasures of the Web. Name notwithstanding, it plays not only Beethoven, but also a wide range of familiar and challenging classical pieces from 7:30 AM until midnight, local time. This station also puts "*nouveau* popular" classical operations to shame by playing a goodly number of long pieces—and playing them all the way through, without interruption. The limited announcements and ads are delivered in Spanish, usually by station announcers in an unobtrusive and dignified manner.

WBOQ, Gloucester, Massachusetts, www.wbach.com/getreal.html. Familiar classical favorites along with movie music and other light quasi-classical fare from one of New England's oldest fishing communities. Pleasant background fare for when you are tickling your PC's ivories.

WCLV, Cleveland, Ohio, www.wclv.com. This Lutheran commercial station airs better-known classical music, along with religious programs (mostly on Sunday) and some other offerings. Note that this station uses streaming software from Shockwave, Audioactive and NetShow—nearly everything but RealAudio!

WFMT, Chicago, www.radio.broadcast.com/radio/Classical/WFMT. Here is where you get the best winds from the Windy City, some of the finest classical offerings anywhere. This popular commercial station airs ads and news in addition to classical music of all sorts. In principle the Metropolitan Opera's live Saturday broadcasts are blocked out (*see* WQXR, below), but in practice they have been known to sneak through, anyway.

WKSU, Kent, Ohio, www.wksu.kent.edu/live. Excellent ad-free classical programming aired round the clock, along with various NPR information and entertainment programs—all courtesy of Kent State University. Also, *see* "Folk," below.

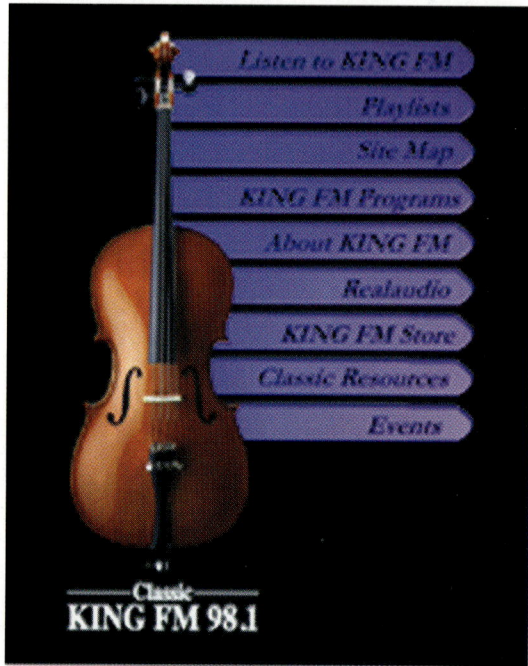

Seattle's nonprofit KING FM was the world's first classical Webcaster. Today, it is considered to be one of the best. KING

WQED, Pittsburgh, www.wqed.org/fm/index.html. Since 1973 this ad-free outlet has aired round-the-clock classics, now including featured orchestras (Pittsburgh's is on Tuesday) and Karl Haas' "Adventures in Good Music" teachings weeknights. Sunday includes the Pittsburgh Symphony once again, along with an evening opera. One of the best, with technology to match.

WQXR, New York, www.classicalinsites.com/live/wqxr. Few things in New York stay constant over the better part of a century, but *The New York Times'* WQXR is among them. This award-winning station carries the Metropolitan Opera live Saturdays—no blocking here!—along with ads and the latest from the *Times'* incomparable newsroom.

Part-time Classical

CBC Radio Two—Classics & Beyond, Toronto, Canada, www.radio.cbc.ca/stereo-dir. The CBC is the one institution seemingly every Canadian loves to hate. One of our panelists, an American, used to be a stringer for the CBC. When he was entering at the Calais-St. Stephen crossing some years back, a Canadian immigration official asked what was bringing him into the country. He stated that he was doing some work for the CBC, whereupon he was ordered from his car, then escorted to a roomful of smirking officials and a furious commander who shouted out his grievances against the CBC for a quarter-hour.

For many Americans, used to hearing delightful offerings from the CBC on their AM radios at night, this attitude is incomprehensible, and the Web radio relay of CBC's Radio Two should only serve to add to the mystification. Although not exclusively for the classics, Radio Two brings classical music, including Saturday's live Metropolitan Opera, to the farthest nooks

Miklos Schon, featured pianist of classical music station Accent 4 in Strasbourg, France.
Cybercable

and crannies of Canada—and now, thanks to Web radio, the world. Tune in and enjoy . . . but just don't let on to any Canadian immigration officials!

De Concertzender, Holland, www.concertzender.nl/concertzender/ra. This public radio station doesn't know the meaning of "music lite," making it a favorite stop for serious lovers of classical music of varied types and degrees of popularity. No blackouts and no ads . . . but no commentary in English, either. Concertzender airs the classics except in the wee hours, and stresses Dutch artists.

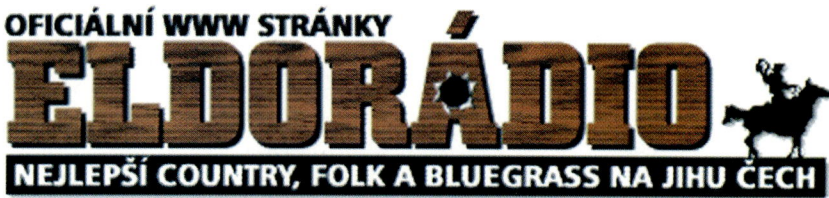

> Eldorádio is where European cowboys Czech in their guns. This iconoclastic East European station features country and bluegrass music, along with native folk music—all surprisingly well done.
>
> Eldorádio

KACU, Abilene, Texas, www.kacu.org. Evenings of ad-free classical music from the public radio outlet of Abilene Christian University.

Philharmonic Radio Taipei, Taiwan, www.prtmusic.com.tw/Voice/index.html. Neither so challenging nor so unconventional as De Concertzender, but also with a classical/jazz format. English announcements, and quite pleasant.

Radio Slovenia, Ljubljana, Slovenia, www.rtvslo.si/radio/indexi.html. Airs a wide variety of symphonies and other pieces, along with news and other non-musical programs in Slovene. Superior audio quality, too.

WFCR, Amherst, Massachusetts, www.wfcr.org. Excellent classical offerings and no ads, but only from 9 AM to 4 PM Eastern Time Monday through Friday and 6 AM to 4 PM Sundays.

WTMI, Miami, www.wtmi.com/realaudio.html. Popular classical music offerings from this commercial station, which shifts over to jazz in the wee hours.

Country

Numerous choices; *see* "Voices from Home" section for specifics. For bluegrass, *see* "Folk," below.

Ethnic

If you hail from another part of the world, or simply wish to keep in touch with an ancestral homeland or country you've visited, Web radio opens up vistas never before available. In PASSPORT's "Voices from Home" section there are stations in native tongues and English from over a hundred countries, as well as expatriate transmissions from areas in the United States, Canada and beyond where expats congregate.

Folk

Bluegrass Radio Network, Nashville, Tennessee, www.bluegrassradio.com/audio.html. On-demand—great a-pickin' and a-fiddlin' bluegrass shows, hosted by Terry Herd.

Eldorádio, České Budějovice, Czech Republic, broadcast.eldoradio.cz. Pleasant mix of folk, bluegrass, country and popular romantic ballads in Czech and English. Czech it out.

WFCR, Amherst, Massachusetts, www.wfcr.org. "Valley Folk" with Susan Forbes Hansen is a fine catch each Saturday from 9 PM to midnight, Eastern Time.

HO*T FM features German *jugendlich* freeform music with American attitude. Shown, the station's exuberant staff.
HO*T-FM

WKSU, Kent, Ohio, www.wksu.kent.edu/live. Kent State University airs a worthwhile program of folk music Friday, Saturday and Sunday evenings from 8 PM to midnight, Eastern Time.

WWOZ, New Orleans—*see* Part-time Jazz, below. Nonprofit WWOZ's format includes outstanding Cajun, zydeco and other forms of indigenous Louisiana music.

Freeform/Diversified

"Traditional" freeform is all but dead, victim of our comfortable *société de consommation*, although in GenX incarnation it does crop up on FM and Web radio at some university stations. Problem is, it is hit-and-miss except at a precious few outlets, such as the University of Pennsylvania's creative WXPN-FM, which has pitiful local ratings (but is not on Web radio).

bFM, Auckland, New Zealand, ra-systems.co.nz/~bfm/cool.html. Auckland University's station, catering to young-nouveau tastes. Eclectic, but is sometimes diminished by nattering.

GoGaGa, Boulder, Colorado, www.gogaga.com. Assorted music for the mind searching for the soul, with periodic repeats. Live and on-demand, so there's virtually no end of choice. The same group also turns out **Radio M** at www.radiom.com.

HO*T FM, Hof, Germany, www.hot-fm.de. There is *inter alia* "new freeform" for youth and "classic freeform" for boomers. HO*T is new and rock/pop-oriented—almost a worthy American station, but with a German accent.

KCIA, Valencia, California, shoko.calarts.edu/~kcia. It doesn't get more freeform than this self-described "no format radio" from the California Institute of Arts. Don't ask for a description—check it out for yourself!

KMNR, Rolla, Missouri, www.umr.edu/~kmnr/raudio. Youth freestyle from the University of Missouri.

KOTR—*see* Rhythm 'n' Blues, below.

KPIG, Freedom, California, www.kpig.com. Back in the late Sixties, there was a brief period of freeform "underground" FM radio. One of the longest-lived of these was KFAT in, unsurprisingly, the San Francisco Bay area. That went belly up, but shortly thereafter much of the KFAT gang wound up on KPIG-FM in tiny Freedom, well south of the Bay-area listenership.

To increase their audience, they added Webcasting—the first commercial station in the world to do so—and it worked. Soon, their Web audience became significant, gravitating to KPIG's unpredictable mix of folk, classic rock, political ballads, old-time country and irreverent politics that somehow flowed seamlessly.

Alas, few advertisers materialized, and most that did were local and irrelevant to the Web audience. So the owners recently adjusted the format closer to that of a typical classic rock station. The operative word is "closer," because there's still no confusing KPIG with any other station on the air. But the change clearly shows. As one listener lamented, "They've replaced poetry with prose."

Oink.

WEBK, Killington, Vermont, www.webk.com/wlisten.shtml. Alternative rock, Southern rock, classic rock, adult rock, country, blues and Cajun constitute the main types of music found on this fun-loving commercial outlet located in the heights of Vermont's prime ski country.

WEBR, Fairfax, Virginia, www.axsamer.org/webr/listen.html. A rich variety of offerings, including classic foreign rock, alternative rock, metal, folk, blues, gospel and country from this all-volunteer cable radio outlet.

WFMU, New York, www.radio.broadcast.com/radio/Public/WFMU. Only New York could come up with something this offbeat that also has a strong listener following across the generations. Try listening to an evening of songs dealing with putrefaction, for starters . . .

WMUC, College Park, Maryland, www.wmuc.umd.edu/real. Youth freeform from this, one of two University of Maryland radio outlets. Their wide range of offerings includes techno, punk, world music, jazz and DC-area bands.

WNTI, Hackettstown, New Jersey, www.wnti.org/index2.html. More conventional than most freeform stations, with relatively wide generational appeal. Still, it's genuine freeform, from Centenary College.

WPTS, Pittsburgh, Pennsylvania, www.wpts.pitt.edu/realaudio. Round-the-clock diversified programming from the University of Pittsburgh includes reggae, jazz, folk, rap, metal and world music.

WRCT, Pittsburgh, Pennsylvania, www.wrct.org. Freeform programming 24 hours from Carnegie Mellon University focuses on the latest rock styles, but also goes back to jazz and earlier styles, including big band. Uses only Audioactive and Shockwave, not RealAudio.

WRNR, Annapolis, Maryland, www.wrnr.com. Yes, Virginia, there is freeform radio on the East Coast. Rock, blues, jazz, reggae, folk and the like are on WRNR's no-playlist menu of live and on-demand offerings. Some technical hiccups, but these should clear up over time.

WSIA, Staten Island, New York, wsia.cuny.edu. This sounds like a college station, and it is, from the College of Staten Island. Cuts run the gamut from Leadbelly-type folk and surfing music to ska, jungle and techno.

Greek

WHCI, Chicago, www.hellenicradio.com/live.html. This ethnic Greek station includes selections of traditional Greek music. Sources for modern Greek music can be found under "Greece" in PASSPORT's "Voices from Home" section.

What do you expect from Killington, Vermont? A party station, of course! Jock Dan Spencer gets set for another day of revelry at "The Mountain," WEBK-FM. WEBK

You can hear Janet—her *nom de microphone*—over Annapolis' eclectic WRNR each Saturday from 10:00 AM to 3:00 PM, Eastern Time. She's also a writer and graphic artist, and loves steamed crabs. "I can never get enough traveling, and I sing in the car," she confesses. WRNR

Hawai'ian

Da Coconut Wireless, San Jose, California, www.punawelewele.com/cocontyrls or www.kkup.com. "Pau Hana Friday" Hawai'ian gathering starts at 7:00 AM Pacific Time Fridays.

Internet Radio Hawai'i, Kailua, Oahu, hotspots.com/irhmusic2.html. On-demand weekend "Music to Cruise By" shows, with modern and traditional Hawai'ian music, along with laid-back Hawai'ian news and an Island activities calendar.

KPOA, Lahaina, Maui, www.mauigateway.com/~kpoa/page6.html. Billed as airing "the island sounds of Hawai'i," this is Web radio's best bet for live contemporary Hawai'ian music.

Jazz

Full-time Jazz

JAZZY, Dallas, Texas, www.broadcast.com/radio/internal/asx/jazzy. The in-house jazz outlet of Web radio network broadcast.com. Uses NetShow.

NetRadio Jazz, Minneapolis, www.netradio.net/classical. Think of this as an on-ground airline audio system, but with all your channel choices being jazz—horns, lounge, divas, café, acid and so forth . . . but no Dixieland or New Orleans categories. It's a great idea as far as it goes, especially as you hear no ads.

☞ *Catch:* Your PC may wind up downloading NetRadio's on-screen ads, which on slower machines chews up so many resources that the music hiccups. *Solution:* Get RealAudio working, then exit the browser.

Radio Free New Orleans, www.neworleansonline.com/rfno.htm. Every day, this site features a different type of New Orleans jazz, sans ads, plus Mardi Gras specials. The station appears to be expanding its offerings. Also, *see* WWOZ, below.

Hawai'i's KPOA-FM broadcasts up-to-date island sounds for those who are 25 and over. It claims to be the first choice among visitors to Maui—not surprising, considering how swell it sounds. KPOA

WBGO, Newark NJ, data.jazzcentralstation.com/wbgo/index.asp. Arguably the planet's best jazz FM station, ad-free WBGO is "must" listening for anyone halfway serious about this art form. It's proof positive that not all American public radio is becoming gooey and safe.

Part-time Jazz

Philharmonic Radio Taipei, Taiwan, www.prtmusic.com.tw/Voice/index.html. Don't let the name or location fool you. Yes, this is primarily a classical music station, and yes, it's from Taiwan. But if great jazz focused on the fifties through seventies is what you want to hear, this station is hard to beat when you tune it at the right times. Announcements are in Chinese, but the performers' names are easily intelligible.

WFCR, Amherst, Massachusetts, www.wfcr.org. Old and new American jazz is aired Monday through Thursday evenings from 8 PM to midnight, with international jazz being offered Friday evenings from eight to eleven on this nonprofit station.

WPFW, Washington, DC, capacity.com/wpfwradio. This Pacifica-owned public radio outlet airs real jazz, nothing like the smooth variety, along with blues, world music and plenty of information on issues of interest to political liberals.

WTMI, Miami, www.wtmi.com/realaudio.html. Mainly a commercial classical music station, but at midnight it changes, like a hip Cinderella, to a snazzy jazz format.

WWOZ, New Orleans, www.radio.broadcast.com/radio/Jazz/WWOZ. What kind of jazz did you expect from New Orleans, anyway? A great find among ad-free Web radio stations, with much more than just jazz to commend it. Also, *see* Radio Free New Orleans, above.

Smooth Jazz

"Smooth" jazz may lack cachet, but most stations airing it actually manage to support themselves commercially.

KIFM, San Diego, California, www.kifm.com.

KMJZ, Minneapolis, Minnesota, www.kmjz.com/live.html.

Radio Slovenia offers quite a bit of classical music over the "3 Program." Its other two networks offer a wide variety of national programming, including delightful Slovenian folk music. RTV Slovenija

28 PASSPORT TO WEB RADIO

Smooth-jazz hosts Maria Jannello, Norman B. and Alicia Kaye of Florida's WSJT report from the grand opening of Disney's Animal Kingdom. WSJT

KTNT, Oklahoma City, www.ktnt.com.

WAHD, Wilson, North Carolina, www.nc.ndl.net/~wahdfm/wahd01.html.

☞ Requires download of "Destiny" software.

WFSJ, St. Augustine, Florida, www.radio.broadcast.com/radio/Jazz/WFSJ.

WHCD, Auburn, New York, www.radio.broadcast.com/radio/Jazz/WHCD.

WJJJ, Pittsburgh, Pennsylvania, www.broadcast.com/radio/jazz/wjjj. Uses NetShow.

WJZT, Tallahassee, Florida, www.radio.broadcast.com/radio/Jazz/WFSJ.

WLVE, Tampa, Florida, www.radio.broadcast.com/radio/Jazz/WLVE.

WSJT, Lakeland, Florida, www.radio.broadcast.com/radio/Jazz/WSJT.

WSMJ, Richmond, Virginia, www.wsmj.com/listenlive.htm.

Jewish

Israel—*see* **"Voices from Home."** For legal and other reasons, Israeli Webcasting has had a shifting cast of players. However, two live broadcasters likely to stay active are **Radio 100FM**, which carries Kol Israel's Reshet Bet news, and **Radio Tel Aviv**, which airs other news. All in Hebrew, of course, and Radio 100FM is best with a modem of 33.6k or better.

Radio J, Paris, France, www.cyberj.com/info/index.html. On-demand news, in French, of the Diaspora and Israel.

Kids

NetRadio Kidz, Minneapolis, Minnesota, www.netradio.net/kidzradio. Kids get plenty of TV shows, but where are their radio stations? NetShow to the rescue, with enough kids' news, music, games and animations to keep children and their parents happy.

☞ *Catch:* Your PC may wind up downloading NetRadio's on-screen ads, which on slower machines chews up so many resources that the music hiccups. *Solution:* Get RealAudio working, then exit the browser.

Latino/Hispanic

There are numerous Spanish-speaking stations on Web radio, but most are contemporary and predictable. Too, connections are not yet always what they could be. To sample these offerings, turn to

PASSPORT's "Voices from Home" section, looking under Mexico, Puerto Rico, Venezuela and so on.

La Exitosa, Panama City, Panama, www.sinfo.net/exitosa. Fine music, but ads aplenty.

WRTO, Miami, www.wrto.com. Cuban rhythms don't get much better than this, *La 98 FM* from Little Havana.

Mexican

XEMU, Piedras Negras, www.la-rancherita.com.mx. Ranchera is arguably the finest style to emanate from Mexico's vibrant musical heritage. This commercial station, also known as *"La Rancherita,"* airs both lively and romantic ranchera music live from the Rio Grande border. *¡Ay, yi, yi, yi!*

XERC, Mexico City, radiocentro.com.mx/elfonografo. Great nostalgic Mexican songs carried on the Web by the Radio Centro group, which as of presstime has had a dismal technological track record with Webcasting. Try listening, anyway—the delightful music is well worth it.

Brazil is chockablock with Web radio stations beyond those of interest to a general worldwide audience. Some are worth seeking out for their modern Brazilian music, others for live coverage of *futebol* games.
R. Liberdade

Middle Eastern/Turkish—Islamic

All but absent from American airwaves are the haunting musical refrains from Arab, Persian, Turkish and other Islamic cultures of the Near and Middle East. Web radio to the rescue!

☞ Calls to prayer and other religious programs tend to be carried within the program day of live transmissions from these and other Islamic stations (*see* "Voices from Home" section for details).

NETRADIO: HOW MUSIC SHOULD BE (ALMOST)

Imagine surfing up and down the FM dial, getting channel after channel of nothing but the music you want. Without commercials, without deejay chatter.

Howard Johnson's 48 Flavors

Well, turn off your grandfather's radio and click onto Minneapolis' NetRadio (www.netradio.net), where you can choose from such flavors as jazz, Christian, classical, country, dance/urban, electronica, kidz, modern rock, New Age, pops, vintage rock and world music.

Once the screen comes up for the type of music you've selected, you get to narrow the choice down further to what you *really* want. For example, click on "vintage rock" in the main menu, then in the next menu you get to choose from general vintage, vintage reggae, British invasion, guitar heroes, hard rock, party rock and surf's up.

Take "party rock." Click on this, and you get blasted by pounding rock-'n'-rolldies from the fifties and sixties—the greatest, sweatiest dance music to ever come from a roadside Wurlitzer. As Little Richard once exulted, this is the "healing music—it makes the blind see, the lame walk, and the dumb and deaf hear and talk"!

> **Healing music—it makes the blind see, the lame walk!**
>
> —Little Richard

Stuck Groove

Ah, but there's a catch. After an hour or so, you start hearing the same stuff again and again. You'd better be having a mighty short affair if you're relying on NetRadio's party rock for entertainment.

Next day? You guessed it. How many times can you hear "Johnny B. Goode" before wanting to throw your modem out of the window?

Still, NetRadio points to the electrifying future of Web radio—loads of you-choose-'em offerings that ordinary radio can't begin to match. *Laissez les bons temps rouler!*

Egyptian Radio, Cairo, Egypt, www.sis.gov.eg/realpg/html/adfront9.htm. Some great on-demand offerings of Egyptian music, including Laila Murad and the legendary Om Kolthum.

Muslim Television Ahmadiyya, College Park, Maryland, alislam.org/audio. Not meant to be an entertaining site, MTA is unusual in that it airs Islamic religious and educational fare in English, as well as various languages of established Islamic societies.

Radio Casablanca, Rabat, Morocco, www.maroc.net/rc/boite.html. This site, alas, is not live. However, it has an excellent menu of on-demand indigenous Moroccan music that's great to work or study by. Superior fidelity, too.

Radio Tunis, Tunisia, www.radiotunis.com/live.html. A rich variety of excellent on-demand traditional and modern Tunisian music, plus similar music carried over Radio Tunis' live Arabic-language programming.

Sultanate of Oman Radio & TV, Muscat, Oman, www.oman-tv.gov.om. Unusually pleasant Arab music, along with a mixed bag of non-musical programming. As of presstime, this station's Web server was plagued with various technical shortcomings, but that should improve over time.

☞ If clicking on "Worldwide" doesn't get results, then try "Oman." The resulting audio may be hiccupy, but at least it works.

TGRT, Istanbul, Turkey, www.tgrt-fm.com.tr/TgrtSag.htm. Traditional Turkish music from the Ottoman homeland, but beware audio distortion.

TURADYO, Toledo, Ohio, www.turkiye.org/radyo. Delightful traditional Turkish music, including with video.

Arab music has almost no exposure in the West outside émigré circles. One of the best ways you can experience it firsthand is to tune to stations from that part of the world, including Radio Tunis from North Africa's Maghreb. RTV Tunisienne

Native American

Mohawk Nation Radio, Tyendinaga ON, Canada, www.suckercreek.on.ca/kweradio/audio1.htm. When is the last time you listened to a Mohawk Indian radio station? Or *any* Native American station? Fortunately, this Ontario FM outlet (105.9 MHz) now has a small but growing number of on-demand audio clips, and—best of all—hopes to go live in the coming months.

New Age

Given the popularity of New Age topics and music, it's surprising more of it isn't heard on the airwaves outside the occasional slot on public radio stations ordinarily devoted to other formats. Fortunately, Web radio provides a New Age option whenever you

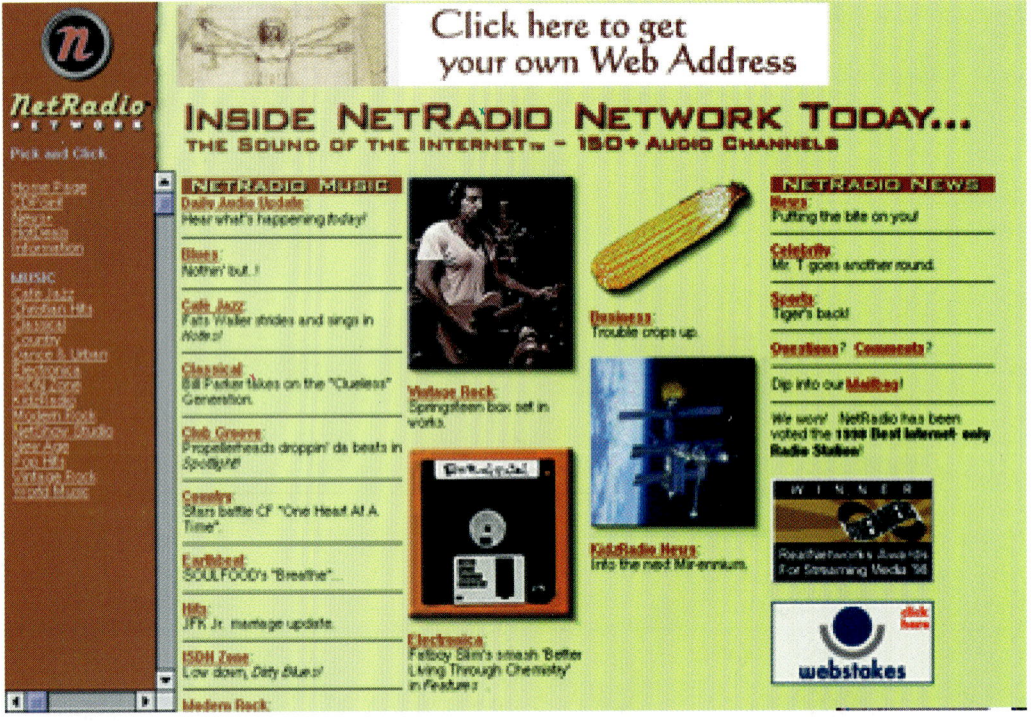

NetRadio (*see* page 30) points to radio's future. It allows you to select exactly what you want, when you want it—and you don't have to put up with ads or chatter. NetRadio

want to listen, instead of when others want you to listen.

NetRadio New Age, Minneapolis, www.netradio.net/newage. Think of this as an on-ground airline audio system, but with all your channel choices being New Age—musical starstreams, nature sounds and so on. It's a great idea, especially as you hear no ads.

☞ *Catch:* Your PC may wind up downloading NetRadio's on-screen ads, which on slower machines chews up so many resources that the music hiccups. *Solution:* Get RealAudio working, then exit the browser.

News—Business

In addition to these stations dedicated to business and financial news, summaries and analyses are widely available at various times of the day from any number of major news outlets shown in PASSPORT's "Voices from Home," including the BBC World Service (*see* below).

iBNN, Ottawa, Ontario, Canada, www.koolcfra.com. Internet Business News Network reports.

WBBR, New York, www.bloomberg.com/wbbr/index.html. Business, financial and commodities news and analysis, along with national, international and sports news. All from Bloomberg News Radio, one of the world's most thorough and respected sources for economics news.

World Talk Network, Houston, Texas, www.broadcast.com/shows/worldtalk. Inspirational entrepreneurial messages and information.

News—International

One of the great features of Web radio is to be able to get local news, sports and weather from nearly any hometown within the United States, along with many places beyond.

But that's only the beginning. Web radio also carries international and regional news from several countries, including the world's finest source of world news: the BBC World Service. These global stations are heard worldwide not only on Web radio but also, along with numerous others, over shortwave radio. (For details, check out the annual book, PASSPORT TO WORLD BAND RADIO at www.passport.com.)

BBC World Service, London, United Kingdom, www.broadcast.com/bbc. Heads of state regularly interrupt official meetings to hear the BBC's newscasts on the hour. For generations, this prestigious 24-hour service has provided the finest in news reporting and credible analysis throughout the world. It is "must" listening for anybody whose perspective on the day's events extends beyond the parochial.

CNN Audioselect, Atlanta, Georgia, www.cnn.com/audioselect. Five CNN networks, including sports, are offered in case you are away from your TV.

Protestant

Protestant religious programming, especially evangelical, abounds on the Web, just as it does over regular airwaves. Look within the "Voices from Home" section, particularly under USA, for specifics on transmissions in English.

Rock—New/Alternative/Electronica/Hip-Hop/Ska/Techno

You don't need Web radio for most of this. But you do need it to be on top of what's emerging, to get real diversity, or to get a juicy earful without a wasteland of obnoxious ads. For the more standard commercial FM offerings, roll your eyeballs over PASSPORT's "Voices from Home" section.

Bandit, Stockholm, Sweden, www.bandit.se/live/index.html. Sounds like an American station in Swedish, but the new rock playlist is distinctive.

bFM—*see* Freeform, above.

Couleur 3, Lausanne, Switzerland, www.rsr.ch/couleur3/index.asp. Hip-hop and techno cuts and interviews oriented to French-speaking cultures in Europe and Africa.

If you like your news "lite" and parochial, turn to any TV newscast. But for *real* news, the way God intended it to be, turn to the BBC World Service. It has no equal, and its entertainment is just awesome.
BBC Photograph Library

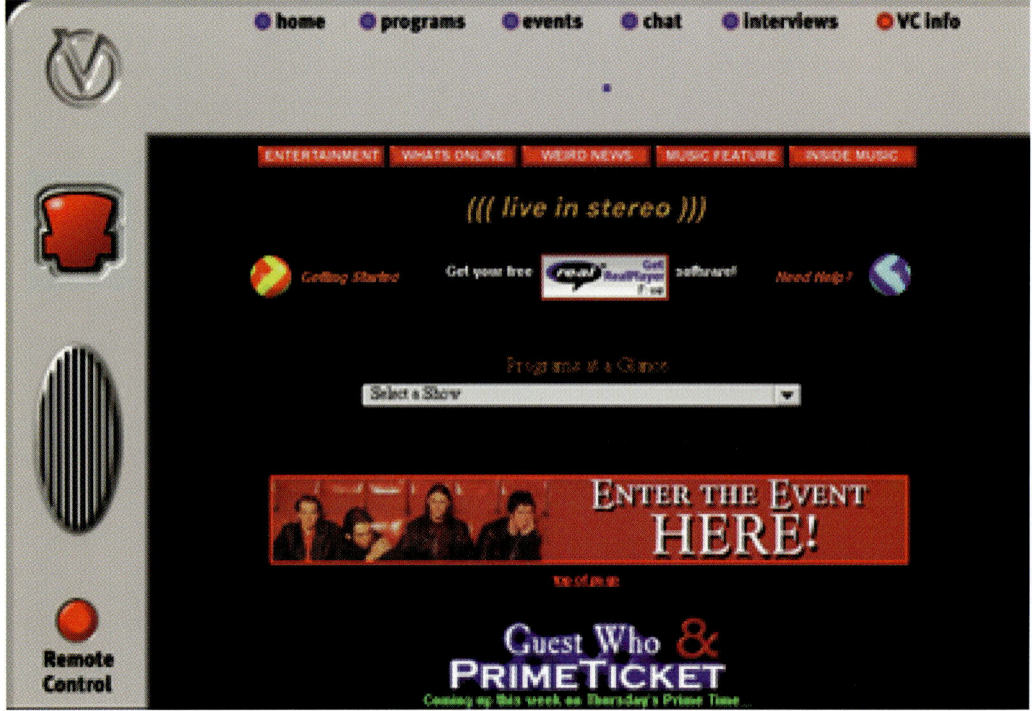

Toronto's "Virtually Canadian" Website serves up a lively diet of Canadian-oriented alternative and kindred music, along with news of rock-related events.
Virtuallycanadian.com

DASDING, Baden-Baden, Germany, www.dasding.de/real. New and urban music in English and German, with the title being played displayed on-screen. Much music, little chatter . . . and never boring.

iMusic, Seattle, Washington, imusic.com/radio. Three great on-demand channels of alternative, electronica and indie rock.

KBUX, Columbus, Ohio, kbux.ohio-state.edu/real.html. Round-the-clock ad-free indie rock, hip-hop and electronica from a basement studio at Ohio State University.

Metro FM—*see* African, above.

Music Bird, Tokyo, www.tfm.co.jp/MB. Yes, the Japanese can party with the best of us, and this "bird" station—satellite radio and TV are big in Japan—serves up a stream of great techno and hip-hop offerings, along with other cuts, albeit with some local wee-hours breaks.

NetRadio Electronica, Minneapolis, Minnesota, www.netradio.net/electronica. Think of this as an on-ground airline audio system, but with all your channel choices being related to electronica—ambient, bhangra, industrial, sci-fi, techno and so on. It's a great idea, especially as you hear no ads.

☞ *Catch:* Your PC may wind up downloading NetRadio's on-screen ads, which on slower machines chews up so many resources that the music hiccups. *Solution:* Get RealAudio working, then exit the browser.

Radio Planet FM, Milan, Italy, www.radioplanet.it. Techno and kindred styles around-the-clock, with Italian panache and announcements.

Triple J, Sydney and Victoria, Australia, www.abc.net.au/triplej/listen.htm. Creative playing is coming from "down thar," and there's no better way to keep abreast of the bleeding edge of Australian rock than by tuning to Triple J. At least 35 percent of the music is pure Aussie, and there are interviews as well as live performances.

☞ Triple J is testing out Webcasting, so there is a chance that when the test is over it could vanish from the cyberwaves.

Virtually Canadian (VC), Toronto, Canada, www.virtuallycanadian.com. If you're looking for the stereotypical slow-mo "Canada Culture" site, don't click here. This satellite/Web station kicks butt with a nonstop diet of live and archived alternative rock with Canadian hormones.

WMUR, Milwaukee, Wisconsin, www.mu.edu/stumedia/wmur/index.html. Alternative rock, rock, techno, metal and hip-hop share the limelight with reggae and classical Monday through Friday from 9:00 AM to 4:30 PM Central Time. Some ads, even though WMUR is the official outlet of Marquette University.

WRUV, Burlington, Vermont, www.uvm.edu/~wruv. Ad-free ska, metal, hip-hop, hardcore, folk, reggae and more emanate from this outlet of the University of Vermont.

Rock—Oldies & Classic

Hundreds of choices; *see* PASSPORT's "Voices from Home" section for the A–Z.

WRUV-FM is squirreled away in the basement of the student center at the University of Vermont. A nonprofit station, it airs music to suit the up-to-the-minute tastes of college students on campus and beyond.
University of Vermont

Roman Catholic

WEWN, Birmingham, Alabama. Lots of Hail Marys and other prayers, monastic chants, and other sober Catholic fare reflecting the outlook of no-nonsense Mother M. Angelica, Our Lady of the Angels Monastery and the Eternal Word Foundation. In the continuum of Catholic broadcasting, traditionalist WEWN is the polar opposite of the freewheeling Rádio Diocesana, below.

Rádio Canção Nova, Cachoeira Paulista, Brazil, www.fastnet.com.br/tvcn/rcn_ao_vivo.html. Evangelical and educational Catholic charismatic programming in

Portuguese, with the objective of fostering peace, love and justice. Getting live audio is a hit-and-miss affair.

Rádio Diocesana, Cachoeiro de Itapemirim, Brazil, www.dci.org.br/aberturad2.htm. Catholic radio is usually, well, catholic . . . thoughtful stuff for the soul and mind. Apparently somebody threw out the rule book in the coastal Brazilian state of Espírito Santo. Rádio Diocesana, operated by the Diocese of Cacheiro de Itapemirim, mixes the usual religious homilies with Brazilian popular and rural music—and lots of ads. All in Portuguese, of course, and the audio sounds as if it's taken off-air. But it is a neat way to experience one of the lighter, more pragmatic corners of worldwide Catholicism.

Radio Ognjišèe, Ljubljana, Slovenia, www.ognjisce.si/ognjisce/iradio. Amid the religious programming in Slovene is some pleasant traditional Slovenian, Catholic and popular music. Sometimes a connection can't be made, especially weekends.

Vatican Radio, Vatican City, www.wrn.org/vatican-radio/audio.html. The official multilingual news voice of the Holy See.

Voice of Charity Radio, Jounieh, Lebanon, www.radiocharity.org.lb/main.htm. Operated by the Maronite Lebanese Missionary Congregation, this station broadcasts traditional Catholic programming in

California's incredible KOTR, midway along the coast, plays all kinds of good stuff—from R&B to jazz and reggae to folk, with some rock and country thrown in. It's one of the best listens on the Web, from a station with over 10,000 CDs and LPs to choose from.
KOTR-FM

Arabic, as well as English, French, Tagalog and other languages. As of presstime, it's a craps shoot whether the server will actually provide audio at any given moment.

Rhythm 'n' Blues/Gospel

Blues Summit, Dallas, Texas, www.broadcast.com/radio/blues/blues. Nonstop blues round the clock, with a high proportion of relatively recent recordings. Also links to a blues chat group.

KOTR, San Luis Obispo/Cambria, California, www.kotrfm.com. If you're of a certain age and lived where there were large "Negro" communities, you'd tune past the horrible stuff on the main stations and go to the "graveyard" frequencies at the top end of the AM dial. There, you'd find the real article, R&B, the precursor to rock 'n' roll. Today, the high end of the dial is Web radio, and the graveyarder is KOTR. It makes for some of the finest listening anywhere—early and classic R&B, plus new renditions . . . along with old-time and classic gospel.

WMBM, Miami Beach, cirnet.com/stations/wmbm.htm. Today's gospel music, on-demand via CIRnet.

Santa Claus and the Rabbi

NetRadio Holiday Music, Minneapolis, Minnesota, www.netradio.net/holiday. Tired of putting up a Christmas tree or Hanukkah bush, or celebrating your other favorite holiday—only to find that the music of the season . . . isn't? NetRadio solves this problem with a channel that operates only when there's some sort of holiday season to sing about.

XMAS, Dallas, Texas, www.broadcast.com/radio/special_broadcasts/XMAS. Want to feel jolly all year long, or have an excuse to pig out on fruitcake and eggnog? Then tune to broadcast.com's own Christmas

CIRnet's menu ranges from contemporary gospel music (from Florida affiliate WMBM) to the latest in Christian rock. It is among the most visible signs of a growing evangelical presence on the Web. CIRnet

music channel, XMAS. It's year-round, so every day can be Christmas.

Sports

What better way to keep abreast of sports and hear live events than to be able to tune to hundreds of stations throughout the world?

Of course, some are in native tongues, such as the many *futebol* games aired over Brazilian outlets (*go...o...o...o...o...ooool!*). But there are plenty of events in English, such as live rugby from Hit 'n' Country in Toukley, Australia, or NewsTalk ZB in Wellington, New Zealand—as well as collegiate sports from the many universities listed in PASSPORT's "Voices from Home" section. But the single best source for live sports events in North America is . . .

broadcast.com, Dallas, Texas, www.broadcast.com/sports. One can quibble about how useful broadcast.com is for listening to music and the like, but there can be no argument about its coverage of North American sports—professional, collegiate, you name it. The ultimate radio fix for sports junkies!

> **No, Virginia**—Saigon Radio is not in Saigon, or even in Vietnam. Instead, it operates from sunny California, attending to the news and cultural needs of the world's considerable population of expatriate Indochinese. Its on-demand musical offerings are a delight for anyone's ears.
> Saigon Radio

Subcontinental

If you are a fan of Subcontinental music, you can also look under India and Sri Lanka in PASSPORT's "Voices from Home" section for stations which include music, along with a wide variety of other programming.

Internet Ki Awaz, San Dimas, California, www.ipgeek.com/Default.html. On-demand Urdu music from Pakistan.

Navrang Radio, Baltimore, Maryland, www.radio.broadcast.com/radio/international/navrangradio. A rich choice of on-demand music from India.

Pakistan Zone, Toronto. Canada, www.geocities.com/Hollywood/Hills/9291/liveradio.html. On-demand Pakistani music . . . and live cricket!

Tango

Tango Radio, Buenos Aires, Argentina, webs.satlink.com/usuarios/f/fm2000. There are three main religions in Argentina: the Catholic church, *fútbol* and tango, not necessarily in that order. While much of the world thinks of the tango as a dance from a bygone era, in Argentina it is not only a dance and type of music, but a way of living and expressing oneself. Few kinds of music have had this kind of impact for so long, so tune in and see whether this is your *salsa*.

☞ Uruguay's Radio Montecarlo (www.netgate.com.uy/cx20) also has on-demand tangos, but the audio quality is pretty basic.

Vietnamese

Saigon Radio, Westminster, California, www.saigonradio.com. This site links to a number of Vietnamese-language stations with live and on-demand broadcasts, including selections of traditional Vietnamese music.

Prepared by Lawrence Magne, with David Walcutt and Tony Jones.

passport
to world band radio
1 9 9 9

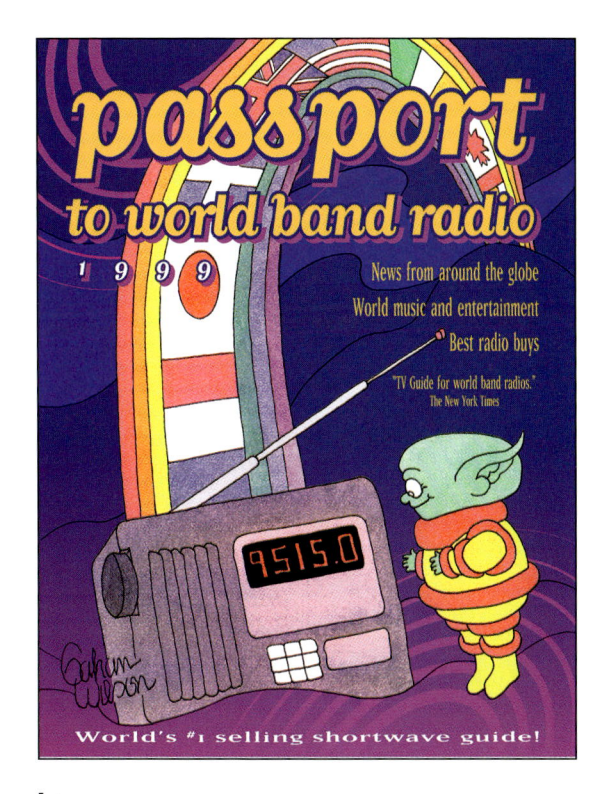

News from around the globe
World music and entertainment
Best radio buys

"TV Guide for world band radios."
The New York Times

World's #1 selling shortwave guide!

Listen... as history unfolds.

Unparalleled news and perspectives, plus every sort of music and diversion: That's world band radio, from as many as 165 countries.

PASSPORT TO WORLD BAND RADIO is jammed with just what you need to eavesdrop on this world: Best and worst radios (PASSPORT REPORTS). Station and Internet addresses and giveaways (Addresses PLUS).

Schedules, too – the way you want them. What shows are on, hour by hour (What's on Tonight)...country by country (Worldwide Broadcasts in English and Voices from Home)... frequency by frequency (the renowned Blue Pages).

With **PASSPORT**, you'll have the world at your fingertips.

Fully revised for 1999.
Over 700,000 copies sold worldwide.
Exceptionally handy for day-to-day use.

"The best. Comparative ratings tell you what's good about the good, bad about the bad, and advertisers be damned."
Outside Magazine

"The bible among shortwavers."
Forbes

"This is the user-friendly book about shortwave radio...very authoritative... very thorough."
BBC World Service

PASSPORT TO WORLD BAND RADIO
The must-have guide to your must-hear world.
0-914941-48-8

Available from dealers and bookstores throughout the United States, Canada and the United Kingdom, or write:

IBS, Box 300, Penn's Park, PA 18943 USA
http://www.passport.com/
e-mail: mwk@passport.com

Voices from Home

Country-by-Country, City-by-City

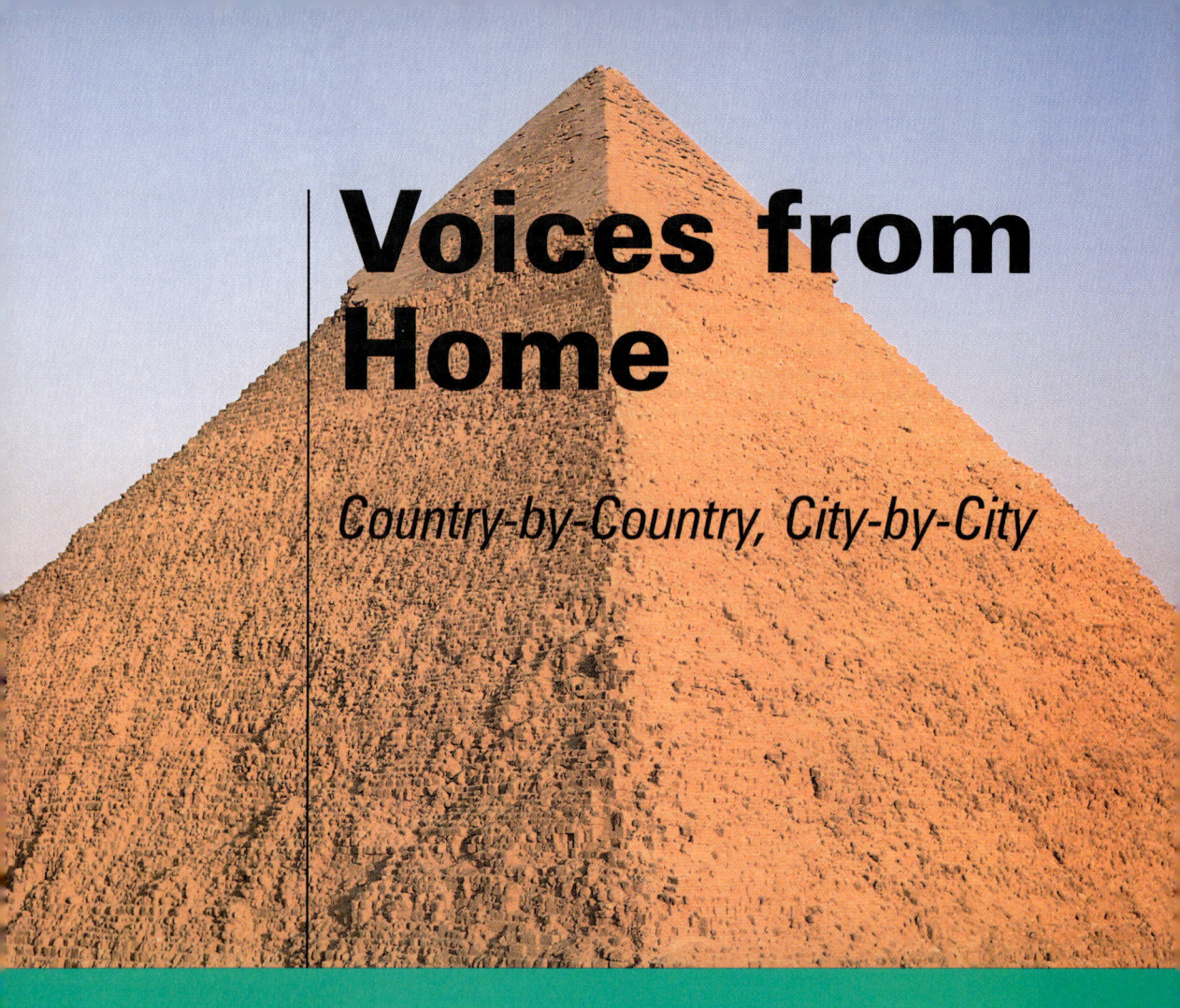

For some, Web radio's musical offerings are merely icing on the cake. Their real interest is in listening to programs aimed at local folks. Voices from home.

"Home" may be where you were raised, or where you went to college or worked. It may be where family or friends live—or a favorite spot, like Tahiti, where you've vacationed. It may even be where you're planning to visit or relocate.

Maybe you just want to eavesdrop, to get a feel for what it's like to be in Lubbock, Texas, or Melbourne, Australia. Or be on-the-spot during a tornado watch around Atlanta, an earthquake in Los Angeles or a hurricane in Miami. Remember that even if a station is knocked off the air, it can sometimes still reach the world via its Web radio server.

Can't make a connection? Overseas stations may have switched off for their early-morning break—see "When Is Teatime in Tahiti" in this PASSPORT to determine stations' local time. Too, some Web stations are silent while their over-the-air transmitters are carrying programs contractually prohibited from being aired over the Web. And some university stations shut down weekends or during school holiday breaks.

Sometimes you can't connect because the Internet is congested, the station's server is busy or down, or its URL (Web address) may have changed. To get around an altered URL, try shortening it by a segment or two between slashes; for example, if www.axolotl.edu/WPOO fails, try www.axolotl.edu.

To avoid having to wait for the download of "clip 1" intro pages found at some Websites, click onto the "next clip" button.

If you keep getting only partial downloads, then a "stall," it sometimes helps to exit the Internet altogether, then "flush out" your computer's swap file by rebooting.

Most Web radio stations operate live, a number offer only on-demand (archival) audio, and some helpful stations offer both. Most listed stations also operate on AM, FM or cable for local coverage, although we've included serious Internet-only stations, as well. Many international stations are not on the Web, but are audible for great distances over world band radio. These are detailed in the annual #1 selling shortwave publication, PASSPORT TO WORLD BAND RADIO.

Transmission languages are those of the country the station transmits from, unless otherwise indicated in the station entry. However, English is becoming increasingly common, even from countries where it is not the native tongue. And most stations air the ultimate in world languages—music!

The Caribbean is more than reggae. Some of the best jammin' music hails from 100 JAMZ in the Bahamas. JAMZ

THE PEOPLE'S CHOICE

ANDORRA—Spanish

Andorra
Ràdio Valira 93.3 MHz	Jingles		www.andornet.ad/r_valira/

ARGENTINA—Spanish

Buenos Aires
Cadena 100	Hits	Severe audio problems.	www.ciudad.com.ar/fr_default.asp
FM Aspen 102.3 MHz	Variety	Limited hours. NetShow.	www.julio-lagos.com.ar/
FM News 98.3 MHz	News/Pop	NetShow.	www.fmnews.com/
Radio Mitre "AM 80"	News/Variety		www.clarin.com.ar/
Tango Radio 90.9	Tangos	On demand site.	webs.satlink.com/usuarios/f/fm2000/

Córdoba
LV3 Radio Córdoba	News Talk		www.powernet.com.ar/lv3/live.htm
Radio Universidad 580 kHz	Variety		www.srt.com.ar/580home.htm

La Plata
Radio FM 92.1 ("La 92")	LA Hits		www.hoy.netverk.com.ar/la92/

Mar del Plata
LU6 Radio Atlántica 1120 kHz	News, Features, and Music	Select "NOTICIAS" and "DISCOTECA".	www.argenet.com.ar/atlantica/

Salta
FM ABC 103.5 MHz	Program Samples	News and Songs.	www.iruya.com/radios/abc/stream.htm

San Nicolás
LT24 Radio San Nicolás 1430 kHz	News Bulletins	On demand site.	www.cablenet.com.ar/lt24/audio.htm

AUSTRALIA—English

Australia Capital Territory
Canberra
2CN 666 kHz	"Audio Postcards"		www.abc.net.au/2cn/postcard.htm

New South Wales
Callaghan
2NUR 103.7 MHz	Community Radio	University of Newcastle.	www.newcastle.edu.au/cwis/ra/

Dirranbandi Bushband of Sydney, Australia, one of the Aussie groups aired over NSW station Hits 'n' Music.

VOICES FROM HOME 43

For the latest trends in Austrian rock, turn to Antenne-Steiermark.
Antenne-Stmk

Sydney

96.1 FM	Rock	NetShow.	www.961.com.au/live.htm
2KY Racing Radio 1017 kHz	Racing/SportsTalk		stellarimages.com.au/2ky/
BFM 88.7 MHz	Adult Contemp.	"coming soon bfm live".	www.bfm.scoastnet.com.au/page5.html
Radio Free Burma	Features/Music	Burmese. On demand.	www.fast.net.au/rfb/
Triple J 105.7 MHz	New Australian		www.abc.net.au/triplej/listen.htm
Triple M 104.9 MHz	Rock		www.village.com.au/airwaves/triplem/mmmsyd/ra.htm
Voice of "Nor Serount"	News/Music	Armenian.	www.ozemail.com.au/~ngcs/

Toukley

Hits 'n' Country FM 94.1 MHz	Country/Rock	aka "Cool Country"	cc.ausweb.net.au/

Queensland

Brisbane

4BBB "B105" 105.3 MHz	Rock		www.b105.com.au/live/
4BC 1116 kHz	Talkback Radio	NetShow.	www.4bc.com.au/audio.asp
4ZZZ "Triple Zed" 102.1 MHz	Progressive	University of Queensland.	www.4zzzfm.org.au/

Innisfail

Radio 4KZ 531 kHz	Hits	"Cairns to Cardwell".	www.4kz.com.au/4kz.html
Kool-FM 98.3 MHz	Rock Mix	Not 24 hours.	www.koolfm.com.au/

South Australia

Adelaide

Austereo Network	News		www.village.com.au/airwaves/austereo/net_nite/net_nite.htm
Radio 5UV 531 kHz	Community	University of Adelaide.	www.adelaide.edu.au/5UV/broadcast.html
SA-FM 107.1 MHz	Rock		www.village.com.au/airwaves/austereo/safm/
Triple M 104.7 MHz	Rock		www.village.com.au/airwaves/triplem/mmmadel/index.htm

Victoria
Melbourne

3AK 1503 kHz	Local Variety/Hits		www.3ak.com.au/main.htm
ABC "Foreign Correspondent"	Ethnic music	On demand site.	www.abc.net.au/foreign/wave.htm
Hitz FM 89.9 MHz	Rock		www.hitzfm.org.au/
KISS 90 FM 89.9 MHz	Dance		www.kiss.sprint.com.au/news/splash.html
Radio Australia	"ABC Live"		www.abc.net.au/ra/elp/elphome.htm
Radio Australia	News & Features		www.wrn.org/stations/abc.html
SRA-FM 94.9 MHz	Eclectic	Testing.	www.sra.org.au/
Triple J	Alternative		www.abc.net.au/triplej/listen.htm

Western Australia
Perth

Triple M 96.1 MHz	Top 40		www.triplem.ii.net/onair.shtml

AUSTRIA—German
Dobl

Antenne Steiermark	Austrian Rock	Click on the loudspeaker.	www.antenne-stmk.at/

Eisenstadt

ORF Radio Burgenland	Pop		www.burgenland.orf.at/ORF/radio.htm

Linz

ORF Radio Oberösterreich	Variety		radio-o.orf.at/
Radio FRO 89.8 MHz	Public Access	Freie Radio Oberösterreich.	www.fro.at/audio/audio.html

Vienna

Antenne Wien 102.5 MHz	Rock	Click "Jetzt auf Antenne".	www.antenne-wien.at/v1/
Der Musiksender 88.6 MHz	Rock		www.886live.at/
ORF Blue Danube Radio	"Today At Six"	English and French.	www.via.at/fobdr/tas.htm
ORF Radio Austria International	News	English.	www.wrn.org/stations/orf.html
ORF Radio Österreich International	Features	On demand downloads.	www.orf.at/roi/gr/gr_home.htm

BAHAMAS—English
Nassau

100 JAMZ	Urban		www.broadcast.com/radio/urban/100jamz/

CANA ONLINE
The Caribbean News Agency Limited (CANA)

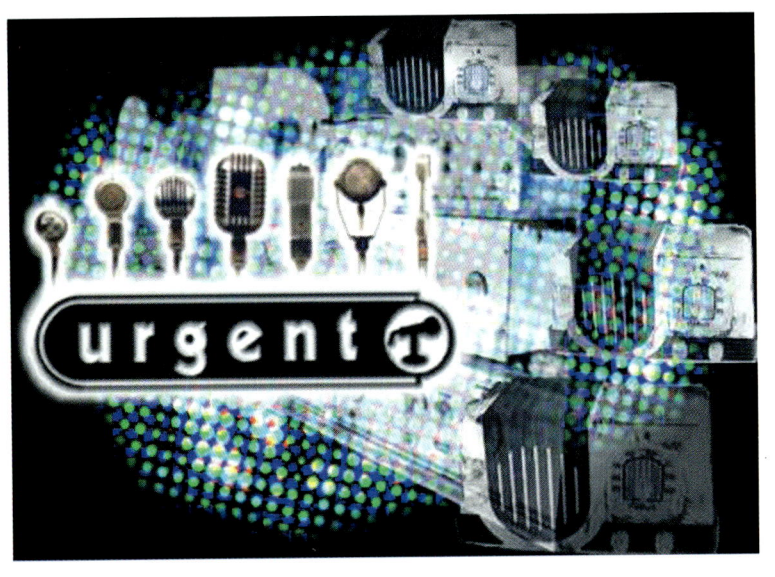

Scrabble buffs: Alternative rocker "Urgent" emanates from University Radio Ghent in Belgium. URG

BANGLADESH—Bangla

Dhaka
Bangladesh Betar	News/Songs	On demand site. Free registration required.	banglaradio.com/

BARBADOS—English

St. Michael
CANA Radio	News	On demand bulletin.	www.cananews.com/

BELGIUM—Multilingual

Borgerhout
Axxes	Freeform	Dutch. NetShow.	www.axxes.be/

Brussels
Radio Vlaanderen Internationaal	News & Features	English and Dutch.	www.wrn.org/stations/rvi.html
RTV Belge "Journal Parlé"	News	French.	www.rtbf.be/jp/

Deinze
Radio Canteclaer 105.1 MHz	Music Samples	Flemish.	www.canteclaer.be/

Ghent
Spitsradio	Adult Contemp.	Dutch.	http://www.spitsradio.be/live.htm
URGent 106.8 MHz	Alternative	Dutch. U. of Ghent.	www.urgent.rug.ac.be/english/live.htm

Liège
Radio Contact 104.5 MHz	French Rock	French. NetShow.	radiocontact.cybernet.be/live.htm

BELIZE—English

Belize City
Love FM 95.1 MHz	Newscast		www.belizenet.com/lovefm.html

(Left) Patrick Jones of Love FM in Belize. (Right) Alain Cristopher, sportscaster at Radio 101 FM, Macapa (Amapa), Brazil.

BOLIVIA—Spanish

Sucre
Radio Loyola 1300 kHz	News Talk	Click "Radio Loyola desde…" Not 24 hours.	www.nch.bolnet.bo/WelcomeTexto.html

BRAZIL—Portuguese

Acre
Rio Branco
Rádio Gazeta 93.3 MHz	Brazilian Pop	Click on the radio.	www.mdnet.com.br/gazetafm/

Alagoas
Maceió
Rádio Gazeta 1260 kHz/94.1 MHz	Variety/Sports	*Two* programs (AM + FM).	www.gazeta-oam.com.br/

Amapá
Macapá
Rádio 101 FM 101.9 MHz	Love Songs	Click on the microphone.	www.brasnet-online.com.br/radio101/

Amazonas
Manaus
Amazonas FM 101.5 MHz	Eclectic Variety		www.amazonasfm.com.br/

Bahia
Salvador
Globo FM 90.1 MHz	EZ Variety		www.gfm.com.br/
Rádio Cidade 101.3 MHz	Pop	Click on the radio.	www.radiocidade.com.br/radioaovivo.html
Rádio Educadora FM 107.5 MHz	News/Info/Music		www.irdeb.com.br/
Rádio Sociedade da Bahia 740 kHz	Pop Variety	Click on radiating tower.	www.tvitapoan.com.br/sociedad.htm

Ceará
Fortaleza
Calypso FM 106.7 MHz	Brazilian Pop		iate.fortalnet.com.br/som/
CBN "AM do Povo" 1010 kHz	News Talk/Sports		www.secrel.com.br/opovo/
Rádio Cidade 95.5 MHz	Rock		www.radiocidade95.com.br/
Rede SomZoom Sat 100.9 MHz	Brazil Pop		www.somzoom.com.br/radio.htm

Distrito Federal
Brasília

CBN Cultura	News/Sports		www.supernet.com.br/cbncultura/audiorel.htm
Sistema LBV 1210 kHz	Religion	"Legião da Boa Vontade".	www.lbv.org/radio/index.html
Rádio 105 FM	Brazilian Rock	Click on "Rádio Internet".	www.correioweb.com.br/servicos/105fm/main2.htm
R. Jornal de Brasília 101.7 MHz	Brazilian Pop	Click on the logo.	www2.opopular.com.br/hpmain.htm
Rádio Planalto AM 890 kHz	Pop Variety	Click on "Rádio Internet".	www.correioweb.com.br/servicos/planalto/main2.htm

Espírito Santo
Cachoeiro de Itapemirim

Rádio Diocesana 960 kHz	Catholic		www.dci.org.br/aberturad2.htm

Goiás
Goiânia

Rádio Araguaia 97.1 MHz	Pop		
Rádio Anhanguera 1230 kHz	Variety	Click on the logo.	www2.opopular.com.br/hpmain.htm
Rádio Executiva 92.7 MHz	EZ Listening	Click on the logo.	www2.opopular.com.br/hpmain.htm
Rádio K 730 kHz	Soccer/Music	Click the RealPlayer icon.	www.kajurunet.com.br/index2.html

Maranhão
São Luís

Rádio Mirante 96.1 MHz	Rock		www.mirante.com.br/radio/

Mato Grosso do Sul
Campo Grande

Rádio Ativa 102.7 MHz	Rock	Click on "aqui".	www.radioativa.com.br/ativaliv.htm

Dourados

Terra FM 101.9 MHz	Rock/Brazilian	NetShow. Click on: "netshow.douranet."	www.terrafm.com.br/netshow/

Minas Gerais
Belo Horizonte

98 FM	Rock & Pop		www.98fm.com.br/index2.htm
Extra FM 103.9 MHz	Hits/Dance		www.itatiaia.com.br/realaudio.html
Rádio 107 FM "Mais"	Rock		www.107fm.com.br/baixo.html
Rádio Alvorada 94.9 MHz	Pop & Soft Rock		www.alvoradafm.com.br/real.htm
Rádio Cidade 90.7 MHz	Religion/Soft Pop		www.fmcidade907.com.br/
Rádio Guarani FM 96.5 MHz	Pop	Click on the loudspeaker.	www.guarani.com.br/index.html
Rádio Inconfidência 100.9 MHz	Brazilian Variety		www.plugway.com.br/inconfidencia/
Rádio Itatiaia 610 kHz	News/Sports/Music		www.itatiaia.com.br/realaudio.html

Congonhas

Rádio Colonial 104.7 MHz	Diverse	Click on the globe.	www.utranet.com.br/colonial/aovivo.htm

Curvelo

Rádio Vereda 95.5 MHz	Rock		www.mrnet.com.br/

Itajubá

Rádio Jovem 98.7 MHz	News/Pop Songs		jovemfm.sulminas.com.br/jovemfm/noticias.html

Paracatu
Rádio Boa Vista FM   Variety   NetShow.   www.lene.com.br/
96.5 MHz

Sete Lagoas
Rádio Musirama 92.1 MHz   Rock   www.mrnet.com.br/news.htm

Viçosa
Rádio 97FM 97.9 MHz   Brazilian Rock   www.vicosa.com.br/radio/
Rádio Universitária   Variety   www.ufv.br/Radio_tv/Radio/
100.7 MHz

Paraná

Curitiba
CBN Paraná 90.1 MHz   News   www.cbn-curitiba.com.br/
Gospel FM 91.3 MHz   Christian   Click on the satellite   www.gospelfm.com.br/
                                               dish.

Londrina
Rádio Folha 102.1 MHz   Pop   folhafm.inbrapenet.com.br/

Maringá
Globo FM 95.5/ 93.3 MHz   Hits/Country   Inactive?   www.netsix.com.br/fm95/
Maringá FM 97.1 MHz   Variety   Click the RealAudio   www.maringafm.com.br/
                                               icon.

Ponta Grossa
FM Mundi 99.3 MHz   Brazilian Pop   www.mundifm.com.br/realaudio.htm

Umuarama
Rádio Ilha Grande   Rhythmic Brazilian   www.ilhafm.com.br/
107.1 MHz

União da Vitória
95 FM 95.1 MHz | **Diverse** | | www.net-uniao.com.br/95/inicio.htm

Pernambuco
Arcoverde
Itapuama FM 95.5 MHz | **Brazilian Pop** | Click "Ao vivo". | sol.arconet.com.br/users/itapuama/

Caruara
Rádio Liberdade 94.7 MHz | **Music Sample** | | marte.netstage.com.br/radio.htm

Recife
Rádio Cidade 95.9 MHz | **Variety** | Click on "aqui". | http://cyberland.recife.softex.br/sbn/cidadecenter.html
R. Jornal do Commercio 780 kHz | **News/Sports** | Click "Radios" graphic. | www2.uol.com.br/JC/servicos/radios.htm
Top FM 106.9 MHz | **Brazilian Pop** | | www.neoplanos.com.br/top.htm

Piauí
Teresina
Meio Norte 99.9 MHz | **Brazilian Pop** | Click on the loudspeaker. | mnnet.mnnet.com.br/

Rio de Janeiro
Campos
Rádio Litoral FM 100.7 MHz | **Brazilian Rock** | | litoral.rol.com.br/

Itaperuna
102 FM 102.5 MHz | **Variety** | | www.102fm.com.br/
Rádio Avahy 103 FM 103.3 MHz | **Pop/Mix** | | www.103fm.com.br/

Nova Friburgo
Rádio Sucesso FM 88.1 MHz | **Hits** | Click on the radio. | www.brasilvision.com.br/sucesso/prin.htm

Petrópolis
Rádio Musical FM 91.1 MHz | **Adult Contemp.** | Click on "radiofm". | www.compuland.com.br/

Rio de Janeiro
FM 98 | **Soft Pop** | Click the logo. | www.globonoar.com.br/
Rádio 1180 AM 1180 kHz | **Pop** | Poor off-air sound. | www.globonoar.com.br/
Rádio Cidade 102.9 MHz | **Brazilian Rock** | | www.barra-da-tijuca.com.br/radio/fra-rad.htm
Rádio Globo AM 1220 kHz | **Variety** | Click *central* Globo logo. | www.globonoar.com.br/
Rádio Globo FM 92.5 MHz | **Rock** | Click the *right* Globo logo. | www.globonoar.com.br/
Rádio Imprensa 102.1 MHz | **Brazilian Pop** | Click on the "RI" logo. | www.imprensa.com.br/clique.htm
Rádio Litoralnet | **Brazilian Pop** | On demand programs. | www.trip.com.br/litoralnet/program.htm
Rádio Tropical 104.5 MHz | **Rhythmic Brazilian** | | tropical.hipernet.com.br/

Rio Grande do Norte
Natal
FM Tropical 103.9 MHz | **Adult Contemp.** | | www.digi.com.br/fmtropical/
Rádio Cidade Natal 94.3 MHz | **Brazilian Pop** | NetShow. | www.radiocidadenatal.com.br/

Rio Grande do Sul
Caxias do Sul
Rádio Caxias 930 kHz | **Variety** | | www.tridio.com.br/ra.html
Rádio Studio FM 93.5 MHz | **Rock** | | www.tridio.com.br/ra.html

Pelotas
Rádio Universidade 1160 kHz	News/Sports	Not 24 hours.	www.ucpel.tche.br/paginas/radio/ru/aovivo.htm

Porto Alegre
Band FM 99.3 MHz	Music, News & Info		www.viars.com.br/band/fm/fm_ra.html
Ipanema FM 94.9 MHz	Rock		www.ipanema.com.br/ipa_ra.htm
Pop Rock 107.1 MHz	Original Variety		www.ulbranet.com.br/poprock/
Rádio Alegria 92.9 MHz	Pop		www.radioalegria.com.br/
Rádio Gaúcha 600 kHz	Variety		www.rdgaucha.com.br:8080/
Rádio Guaíba AM 720 kHz	Variety		www.cpovo.net/radio/

Viamão
Rádio Liberdade 95.9 MHz	Variety	Click on the radio.	www.liberdade-tche.com.br/

Rondônia
Porto Velho
Jovem Pan PVH 96.9 MHz	Classic Rock		www.canal-1.com.br/jovempan/
Rondônia FM 93.3 MHz	News/Variety		www.enter-net.com.br/93fm/

Santa Catarina
Blumenau
Rádio Atlântida 102.7 MHz	Variety	Click the smiling face.	www.atlantidablu.com.br/index.htm
Rádio Atlântida 102.7 MHz	Variety	Alternative URL (direct):	www.bhnet.com.br/banca/radatlsc.ram

Florianópolis
Jovem Pan FM 101.7 MHz	Rock		www.jovempanfloripa.com.br/welcome3.htm

São Paulo
Americana
VOX 90.3 MHz	Brazilian Pop	Click on "OUVIR".	www.vox90.com.br/

Cachoeira Paulista
Rádio Canção Nova 1020 kHz	Catholic		www.fastnet.com.br/tvcn/rcn_ao_vivo.html

Campinas
CBN Cultura 1390 kHz	News		www.supernet.com.br/cbncultura/audiorel.htm

Cruzeiro
Rádio FM Mantiqueira 100.7 MHz	Rock		fast01.fastnet.com.br/mantamfm/

Ribeirão Preto
Clube FM 100.5 MHz	MOR/Pop		www.clube.com.br/real/

São José dos Campos
Band FM 97.5 MHz	Pop/Rock	Click on "aqui".	www.bandvale.com.br/bandra.htm

São Paulo
89 Rockwave 89.1 MHz	Rock		www.rockwave.com/89/ra0.htm
97 FM "Hot Nine Seven" 97.7 MHz	Dance		www.97fm.com.br/princ.htm
Band FM 96.1 MHz	Variety		www.uol.com.br/bandfmsat/
Rádio Bandeirantes 840 kHz	Soccer/Pop/News	Click on "estúdio no ar".	www.uol.com.br/bandeirantes/
Rádio Brasil 2000 FM 107.3 MHz	Rock		asterix.anhembi.br/brasil2000fm/
Rádio CBN 90.5 MHz	News Talk		www.mandic.com.br/radiocbn/
Rádio Eldorado AM 700 kHz	Talk/Info/News	Click on "AM AO VIVO".	www.radioeldorado.com.br/

No wonder the angel is smiling, he's listening to Brazilian rhythms from Rádio Ilha Grande, near the "wild west" border with Paraguay.
R. Ilha Grande

Rádio Eldorado FM 92.9 MHz	Pop	Click on "FM AO VIVO".	www.radioeldorado.com.br/
Rádio Globo AM 1100 kHz	Variety	Click on *left* Globo logo.	www.globonoar.com.br/
Rádio Jovem Pan AM 620 kHz	Pop		www.jovempan.com.br/realaudio.htm
Rádio Jovem Pan FM	Classic Rock		www.jovempanfm.com.br/
Rádio Musical 105.7 MHz	Brazilian Pop		www.uol.com.br/musical/
Rádio Trianon 740 kHz	News	0600-0015 local time.	www2.uol.com.br/trianon/
Tupã Paulista FM 93.9 MHz	Eclectic Brazilian		www.tupanet.com.br/93fm/

BULGARIA—Bulgarian

Plovdiv
Radio Plovdiv 94.0 MHz	Variety	Direct URL:	www.digsys.bg/realaudio/radioplovdiv.ram

Sofia
Darik Radio 98.3 MHz	Rock/News	Direct URL:	http://ns1.netissat.bg:7070/ramgen/da.rm
Radio Vitosha 97.6 MHz	News Bulletins	Select "Tazi stranica s drugi bukvi" for latin text.	www.bulgaria.com:8080/online/realindex.html

CANADA

Alberta—English

Calgary
CFCW 790 kHz	Country		www.cfcw.com/
CJSW 90.9 MHz	Diverse	University of Calgary.	www.cjsw.com/
CKIK "Power 107" 107.3 MHz	Classic Rock		www.power107.com/
CKRY 105.1 MHz	Country		www.country105.com/105ra.html
CKUA 580 kHz Alberta Public Radio	Variety	Not 24 hours.	www.ckua.org/sounds/sounds.htm

Edmonton
CKNG "Power 92" 92.5 MHz	Today's Best		www.power92.com/
CKRA "Mix 96 FM" 96.3 MHz	Adult Contemp.		www.mix96fm.com/
The Edge	Background	Cable company.	www.videotron.ab.ca/Channel_V/Edge/index.html

British Columbia—English
Castlegar
CKQR "BKR" 760 kHz	Best Soft Rock	Boundary Kootenay Radio	www.bkradio.com/

Coquitlam
DENradio (The DEN)	Eclectic Variety	Click on "DENradio" box.	www.denradio.com/

Kelowna
CILK "101 Silk FM" 101.5 MHz	Soft Rock		www.silk.net/realaudio/

New Westminster
CFMI "Rock 101" 101.1 MHz	Classic Rock		www.rock101.com/

Prince George
CIRX "The MAX" 94.3 MHz	New Rock		www.themaxfm94.com/
CKPG 550 kHz	Hits/Talk		www.ckpg.com/real.htm

Surrey
Apna Sangeet Radio	Sikh Community	Hindi and Punjabi.	www.apnasangeet.com/

Vancouver
CFSR "Star FM" 104.9 MHz	Rock		www.starfm.com/
CHKG 96.1 MHz	Ethnic	Chinese.	www.fm961.com/index2.shtml
CHMB 1320 kHz	Talk	Chinese.	www.am1320.com/live/index.htm
CJVB 1470 kHz	International	Multilingual.	www.am1470.com/audio.htm
CKNW 980 kHz	News/Talk		www.cknw.com/
CKZZ "Z-95" 95.3 MHz	Hits		www.z95.com/

Vernon
CICF "Mix 105" 1050 kHz	Hit/Pop Mix		www.mix105.com/collect.html

New Brunswick—English
Saint John
CIOK "K-100" 100.5 MHz	Rock		k100.atlanticwaves.ca/live.html

Newfoundland—English
St. John's
CHMR 93.5 MHz	Magazine/Variety	Memorial U. of Newfoundland.	www.mun.ca/csu/chmr/
CHOZ "OZ FM" 94.7 MHz	Rock		www.ozfm.ca/
VOCM 590 kHz	Talk/Country		www.vocm.com/

Nova Scotia—English
Halifax
CFRQ "Q104" 104.3 MHz	Rock		www.q104.ca/The_Home_of_RockNRoll/

Northwest Territory—English
Inuvik
CBC Western Arctic (CHAK 860)	Variety	English/ Gwich'in Dene/ Inuvialuktun.	www.cbcnorth.cbc.ca/audio.htm

VOICES FROM HOME 53

Iqaluit (Baffin Island)
CBC Eastern Arctic (CFFB 1230) — Variety — English/Inuktitut/Dene. — www.cbcnorth.cbc.ca/audio.htm

Yellowknife
CBC Mackenzie (CFYK 1340) — News & Features — English/Multilingual. — www.cbcnorth.cbc.ca/audio.htm

Ontario—English

Barrie
CFJB "Rock 95" 95.7 MHz — Classic Rock — www.rock95.com/realaudio.html

Burlington
CING "Energy 108" 107.9 MHz — Dance — www.broadcast.com/radio/dance/cing/

Collingwood
CKCB "The Peak FM" 95.1 MHz — Hits — www.thepeak.georgian.net/

Ottawa
Station	Format	Notes	URL
CFRA 580 kHz	News Talk	StreamWorks+RA.	www.cfra.com/
CKDJ 96.9 MHz	Canadian Rock	Algonquin College.	ckdj.comnet.ca/listen.html
CKKL "Kool" 93.9 MHz	Hits & Fun	StreamWorks+RA.	live.koolcfra.com/
iBNN Internet Business News	Business News	StreamWorks+RA.	live.koolcfra.com/

Owen Sound
CIXK 106.5 MHz — Rock/Country — www.radioowensound.com/splashfm.htm

Sarnia
CHOK 1070 KHz — Sports — www.chok.com/realaud.htm

Scarborough
Radio Asia Canada — Music & News — English/Tamil. — www.radioasiacanada.ca/

Thunder Bay
CJSD "Rock 94" 94.3 MHz — Rock — News provided by CKPR. — www.tbsource.com/Entertainment/index.asp

Toronto
Station	Format	Notes	URL
Canadian Thamil Broadcasting	Variety	Tamil. Live program requires subscription.	www.ctbc.com/
CBC Radio News	Live Events		www.radio.cbc.ca/news/live.html
CBC Radio One	News & More		radio.cbc.ca/radio-dir/
CBC Radio Two	Classics & Beyond		www.radio.cbc.ca/stereo-dir/
CFRB 1010 kHz	News/Talk		cfrb.istar.ca/
CFNY "The Edge" 102.1 MHz	New Rock	Direct URL:	204.225.103.237/edge/livefeed.ram
CFTR 680 kHz	All News	On demand site.	www.680news.com/audio/index.html
CHIR-FM 100.5 MHz	Variety	Greek.	www.chir.com/noframe.htm
CHFI "FM98" 98.1 MHz	Rock/Mix	Plays automatically.	www.cybertv.to/chfi/
CHUM 104.5 MHz	Hits		www.chumfm.com/chumfm.asp
CILQ "Q107" 107.1 MHz	Rock	Click on "Q107 LIVE!"	www.q107.com/tio/tio.html
CIRV 88.8 MHz	International	Multilingual.	www.cirvfm.com/
CJCL "The Fan" 590 kHz	Sports		www.fan590.com/realmedia/
CKFM "Mix" 99.9 MHz	Today's Hits		mix.istar.ca/
CKTB "Radio India" 610 kHz	News	Hindu and Urdu. Live broadcasts, evenings.	www.radioindia.com/Page7.html
Pakistan Zone Pakistani Radio	Urdu/Hindi Songs	Urdu. On demand.	www.geocities.com/Hollywood/Hills/9291/liveradio.html

Polskie Radio Toronto	News/Features	**Polish.** On demand site.	www.ituner.com/530AM/prt.htm
The Vietnamese Canadian Broadcasting Group (VNCP)	Features	**Vietnamese.** Many links.	www.vncb.com/
Virtually Canadian	New Music		www.virtuallycanadian.com/
Tyendinaga			
Mohawk Nation Radio 105.9 MHz	Program Samples		www.suckercreek.on.ca/kweradio/audio1.htm
Willowdale			
Democratic Voice of Iran	News & Info	**Farsi.** On demand.	www.dvi.org/engdvi.html

Quebec—French

Montreal

CBC Nord Québec	News/Variety	North Quebec edition of CBC Radio-Canada AM.	www.cbcnorth.cbc.ca/audio.htm
CBC Radio-Canada AM	News/Variety		www.radio-canada.com/radioam/index.html
CBC Radio-Canada FM	Cultural		www.radio-canada.com/radiofm/index.html
Montreal Radio One	News Talk	**English.** Montreal edition of CBC Radio One Live.	www.radio.cbc.ca/regional/Quebec/Montreal/mtlhome.htm
CIBL 101.5 MHz	Quebec Variety		www.cibl.cam.org/CIBL_live.htm
CIEL 98.5 MHz		Check for future plans.	www.ciel.ca/
CIQC 600 kHz	News/Sports	**English.**	www.ciqc.com/realaudio.html
CISM 89.3 MHz	Alternative	University of Montreal.	www.cismfm.qc.ca/
CITE "RockDétente" 107.3 MHz	Pop/Rock		www.rock-detente.com/magazine.shtml

Montreal's CKOI brings Quebec's own brand of rock to the world.
CKOI.

Radio Canada International (RCI)	News & Features	Multilingual.	www.rcinet.ca/

Quebec
CITF "RockDétente" 107.5 MHz	Pop/Rock		www.rock-detente.com/citf/

Saint-Laurent
Net Radio	New Rock	Also **English**.	www.netrad.com/header.htm

Sherbrooke
CHLT 630 kHz	Variety		www.chlt630.qc.ca/lavoie/index2.html

Trois-Rivières
CFOU 89.1 MHz	College Radio	U. of Quebec, T-R.	rage.uqtr.uquebec.ca/

Verdun
CKOI 96.9 MHz	Quebec Rock		www.ckoi.com/

Saskatchewan—English

Regina
CKIT "The Wolf" 104.9 MHz	Rock	6 PM - 9 AM daily.	www.thewolfrocks.com/main.html

Yukon Territory—English

Whitehorse
CBC Yukon (CFWH 570)	News & Features		www.cbcnorth.cbc.ca/audio.htm
CKRW 610 kHz	Variety	"Experimental".	www.ckrw.com/

CHILE—Spanish

Santiago
El Conquistador 91.3	News	On demand site.	openbox.com/conquistador/html/noticias.html
El Conquistador 91.3	Pop		www.elconquistador.cl/
Radio Beethoven 96.5	Classical		www.beethovenfm.cl/RealAudio/index.html
Radio Pudahuel 90.5 MHz	Upbeat Variety	Limited hours.	www.pudahuel.cl/pudahuel/Pages/ra.html
Radio Zero 97.7 MHz	Rock	Click on "SERVER 1".	www.cmet.net/radiozero/
Radioactiva - Chile 92.5 MHz	Rock		www.cmet.net/radioactiva/

CHINA—Chinese

Beijing
China Radio International	News & Features	"Coming soon".	www.cri.cngb.com/

Guangzhou
Pearl River Economic Radio Station ("Radio Guangdong")	News/Variety	**Cantonese**. On demand news, plus 24-hour live audio, in development.	preradio.kol.com.cn/enterprise/preradio/index.htm

Hong Kong
Commercial Radio "CR1"	Variety	**Cantonese**. Click on top "CR1" button.	www.crhk.com.hk/cr1program/index.html
Commercial Radio "CR2"	Variety	**Cantonese**. Click on top "CR2" button.	www.crhk.com.hk/cr2program/index.html
RTHK Radio 1 92.6/94.4 MHz	Variety	**Cantonese**.	www.rthk.org.hk/rthk/live.cgi
RTHK Radio 2 94.8/96.9 MHz	Variety	**Cantonese**.	www.rthk.org.hk/rthk/live.cgi
RTHK Radio 3 567 kHz	Variety	**English**.	www.rthk.org.hk/rthk/live.cgi
Putonghua Channel 621 kHz	Pop Variety		www.rthk.org.hk/rthk/live.cgi
Radio Television Hong Kong	News/Pop	On demand site.	www.iponline.com/rthk/

CHINA (TAIWAN)—Chinese

Taichung

M Radio 105.9 MHz	Variety		www.taichungnet.com.tw/

Taipei

Broadcasting Corp. of China	News/Pop		www.bcc.com.tw/
Educational Broadcasting System	Variety & Features	Two programs. Click text to right of the consoles.	www.ebs.gov.tw/intronew.htm
ICRT "FM 100" 100.7 MHz	Variety	English.	www.icrt.com.tw/live_st2.asp
Philharmonic Radio Taipei 99.7	Classical/Jazz		www.prtmusic.com.tw/Voice/index.html
SINA Radio/Voice of Taipei	News	Requires registration; free but the form is in Chinese.	ww5.sinanet.com/sinaradio/
Super FM 99.1 MHz	Pop		www.superfm99-1.com.tw/super/main.html
Voice of Taipei 91.7/107.7 MHz	Variety	Two programs, not 24 hours? Click "ON AIR."	www.vot.com.tw/

COLOMBIA—Spanish

Bogota

CARACOL Cadena Básica	News/Pop		www.caracol.com.co/webasp2/50vivo.asp
Radio Cadena Nacional (RCN)	Talk		www.rcn.com.co/
Radioactiva 102.9 MHz	Rock		www.radioactiva.com/audio.htm
Radionet	News		www.radionet.com.co/
Super Estación Colombia 88.9	Variety	Audio problems.	www.889.com.co/

Cali

Univalle Estéreo 105.3 MHz	Diverse	Universidad del Valle.	uv-stereo.univalle.edu.co/audio.html

COSTA RICA—Spanish

San José

Radioperiódicos Reloj	News & Opinion	See the "Escuchar" menu.	www.rpreloj.co.cr/noticias.html

CROATIA—Croatian

Osijek

HRT Radio Osijek	Pop		www.hrt.hr/streams/streams_eng.html

Rijeka

HRT Radio Rijeka	News/Pop	Click on the microphone.	www.multilink.hr/radiorijeka/

Sljeme

HRT Radio Sljeme	Variety		www.hrt.hr/streams/streams_eng.html

Split

HRT Radio Split	Pop		www.hrt.hr/streams/streams_eng.html

Zagreb

Hrvatski Radio	Variety/Classical	*Three* national programs.	www.hrt.hr/streams/streams_eng.html
Hrvatski Radio	News & Info	Also **English**. On demand audio archive.	www.hrt.hr/hr/audio/index_eng.html
Radio 101	Daily News	On demand site.	vukovar.unm.edu/r101/audio/aktualni.html

CYPRUS—Greek

Lefkosa

Bayrak Radio Television Corp.	**Variety**	**Turkish.** Two radio programs, AM and FM	brt.emu.edu.tr/

Nicosia

Logos Radio Station	**Greek Pop**	Click on "Logos Radio".	www.logos.cy.net/tv/index.html
Cyprus Broadcasting Corp.	**Music**	*Three* programs.	www.cybc.com.cy/audio.htm
Radio Proto 99.3 MHz	**Local Songs**		www.radioproto.com.cy/

CZECH REPUBLIC—Czech

Ceske Budejovice

Eldorádio 88.4 MHz	**Folk/Country**	"Experimental Broadcast".	live.eldoradio.cz/asc/
Rádio Faktor 104.3 MHz	**Hits**	"Experimental Broadcast".	live.faktor.cz/asc/
Rádio Faktor 2 99.7 MHz	**Oldies**	"Experimental Broadcast".	live2.faktor.cz/asc/

Prague

Czech Radio 1	**News/Variety**		www.rozhlas.cz/
Evropa 2	**Rock**		www.evropa2.cz/live.htm
Radio Prague	**News & Info**	**Multilingual.** "Testing".	www.radio.cz/

DENMARK—Danish

Copenhagen

Copenhagen Calling	**News & Features**	**English.**	www.wrn.org/stations/cph.html
Danmarks Radio	**Features**	On demand site.	www.dr.dk/harddisk/realaudi/
Danmarks Radio Program 1	**Features**		www.dr.dk/p1/lydmur/realaud.htm
Norden This Week	**Nordic News**	**English.**	www.wrn.org/stations/ntw.html

DOMINICAN REPUBLIC—Spanish

Santo Domingo

La Cadena de Noticias	**News**		www.cdnradio.com.do/
La 91 FM	**Adult Contemp.**		home.la91fm.com/

ECUADOR

Cuenca

Super Rock FM 94.9 MHz	**Variety**		www.explore-net.net/949/escucha.html

Guayaquil

CRE 560 kHz	**News/Sports**	Testing.	www.cre.com.ec/index.html

Quito

Radio Centro 97.7 MHz	**Variety**	NetShow. 14:00-17:00.	www.radiocentro.com.ec/rcentro/toc.htm

EGYPT—Arabic

Cairo

Egyptian Radio	**News & Features**	Not 24 hours.	www.sis.gov.eg/realpg/html/adfront9.htm

ESTONIA—Estonian

Tallinn

Eesti Raadio	News	On demand bulletins.	www.er.ee/utoim/uu.html
Eesti Raadio 2	Variety	Click on the blimp.	www.online.ee/raadio.htm
Eesti Raadio "Vikerraadio"	Pop	Not 24 hours.	www.er.ee/viker/frames/vlive.html
Estonian Radio "Raadio Tallinn" (Foreign Languages)	News/Features	**English/Finnish/ Esperanto.** On demand.	www.er.ee/viker/
Radio KUKU 100.7 MHz	Variety	Click on the loudspeaker.	www.zzz.ee/kuku/

FINLAND—Finnish

Helsinki

Finnish Broadcasting Co. (YLE)	News Bulletins	Click "latest newsbulletin".	www.yle.fi/radiouutiset/raamit.htm
Kiss FM 102.4 MHz	Pop	StreamWorks.	www.kiss.fi/
Radio Finland Satellite Audio	News & Features	**Multilingual.** Not 24 hrs.	www.yle.fi/fbc/radiofin.html
Radio Nova	News Headlines	On demand bulletins. StreamWorks.	www.radionova.fi/uutiset/arkisto.html
YLE Radio Finland	News	**Multilingual.**	www.wrn.org/stations/yle.html

Kurikka

Radio Paitapiiska 92.3 MHz	Pop/R&B/Country	Inactive?	www.kauhajoki.fi/paitapiiska/realradi.html

Turku

Radio Robin Hood 91.5 MHz	Discussions	On demand site.	www.radiorobinhood.fi/fin/realaudio.htm

FRANCE—French

Bordeaux

Europe 2 (Bordeaux 94.3 MHz)	**Rock**		www.europe2.atlantel.fr/
SKYROCK 102.8 FM	**French Rock**		www.skyrock.atlantel.fr/
WIT FM	**Rock**	StreamWorks.	www.quaternet.fr:8080/live/ecoute1.html

Lille

Radio Campus Lille 106.6 MHz	**Eclectic**	Click on "Ecoutez nous!"	www-radio-campus.univ-lille1.fr/
Voix FM 92.5 MHz	**French Pop**		www.lavoixdunord.fr/vdn/voixfm/lien_radio.html

Lyon

AFP Audio	**Program Intros**	Download "Chroniques".	www.a2paudio.com/lisons.htm

Neuilly-sur-Seine

Fun Radio	**Rock/Pop**		www.funradio.fr/funlive/home-funlive.html

Paris

Europe 1	**News & Info**	On demand site. StreamWorks+RA.	www.francelink.com/radio_stations/europe1/europe1.html
Europe 2	**Rock**	Click on "LIVE".	www.europe2.fr/newunix.htm
France 3	**Noon News**		france3.axime.com/infos/infos.html
France Culture	**News**	On demand site. StreamWorks+RA.	www.francelink.com/radio_stations/rfc/rfc.html
France Info (Paris 105.5 MHz)	**News Bulletin**		www.radio-france.fr/france-info/infolive.htm
NRJ	**Mellow Rock**	Click on top left NRJ logo.	www.nrj.fr/all_pages.html
Radio FG	**Techno/Dance**	Select "Radio FG" arrow.	www.nirvanet.fr/live/
Radio France International	**News Bulletins**	Also **English**, and **Multilingual**, on demand.	www.francelink.com/radio_stations/rfi/index.html
Radio France Outre-Mer (RFO)	**News**	On demand bulletins.	www.rfo.fr/html/info/information.html
Radio J 94.8 MHz	**Jewish News**	On demand site.	www.cyberj.com/info/index.html
RTL	**News & Info**	On demand site.	www.rtl.fr/
RTL	**Features**	On demand site.	www.francelink.com/radio_stations/rtl/rtl.html
RTL2	**Adult Contemp.**	Live program.	www.rtl2.fr/home.htm
TNC Radio	**"Entire spectrum"**	Also **English, German.**	www.cnam.fr/museum/radio/tnc/index.html

Rodez

12 FM	**News Bulletin**	Download "le flash departemental" in .wav format.	www.allia-com.fr/12fm/sommaire.html

Strasbourg

Accent 4	**Classical**	Requires 32+kb/s connection.	www.cybercable.tm.fr/~yklaiber/accueil_fr.htm
Europe 2 89.5 MHz	**News**	On demand bulletin.	www.sdv.fr/europe2/

Toulouse

Radio Occitanie 98.3 MHz	**Samples**	Occitan.	www.radio-occitania.cict.fr/sons/sons.htm

FRENCH ANTILLES—French

Fort-de-France, Martinique

Radio Caraïbes International	**Caribbean Variety**	Planned. Select "RCI en Live" under MARTINIQUE.	www.rci.gp/

Radio ICS 89.7/103.9 MHz	Rock	"Experimental" site.	www.sasi.fr/ics/direct.htm
Point-à-Pitre, Guadeloupe			
Radio Caraïbes International	Caribbean Variety	Select "RCI en Live" under "GUADELOUPE" heading. Also Creole programs.	www.rci.gp/

FRENCH POLYNESIA—French

Papeete, Tahiti

RFO Tahiti	News Bulletins		www.rfo.fr/html/info/bulletins.html

GERMANY—German

Baden-Baden

DASDING	New Music	Click on "Einschalten!"	www.dasding.de/real
Südwestfunk SWF3, AM & FM	Pop Rock	*Two* separate programs.	www.swf3.de/webradio/

Berlin

R.S.2 94.3 MHz	Old & New Hits	Click on the radio.	www.rs2.de/index2.html
Radio Paradiso 98.2 MHz	Christian	Click on the radio.	www.paradiso.de/english.html
Sender Freies Berlin InfoRadio	News	Click on "Live Radio".	www.inforadio.de/

Brandenburg

FRITZ (Ostdeutschen Rundfunk)	Features	On demand site.	www.fritz.de/radio/sound/index.htm

Cologne

Deutsche Welle	News	Also **English**. On demand site.	www.dmc.net/dw/dw.html
Deutsche Welle	News		www.dwelle.de/dpradio/Welcome.html
Deutsche Welle	News & Info	**Multilingual.**	www.dwelle.de/language.html
WDR Eins Live	Variety	Click on "Real Audio".	www.wdr.de/Hoerfunk/einslive/

Dülmen

Radio Kiepenkerl	Rock		www.nrwo.de/radio-kiepenkerl/online-radio.htm

Frankfurt

Hessischer Rundfunk "HR3"	Variety		www.hr-online.de/hf/hr3/realaudio.html

Hessischer Rundfunk "HR XXL"	New Rock	MPEG Layer 3.	www.liveaudio.de/hr-xxl/
Hit Radio FFH 105.9 MHz	Hits		www.ffh.de/aktuell/index.html
Planet Radio 100.2 MHz	Rock	Click on "ein klick…"	www.planetradio.de/radio.html

Hamburg
Radio Energy (NRJ) 97.1 MHz	Hits		www.energy971.de/

Hof
HO*T FM 94.0 MHz	Freeform		www.hot-fm.de/

Leipzig
Mitteldeutscher Rundfunk	Talk/Info/Features	On demand site. StreamWorks.	mdr.gmd.de/
Radio Top 40-M	Hits		www.top40-m.de/

Magdeburg
Radio Saw 100.1 MHz	Superhits	Click on "Radio hören".	www.radiosaw.de/raeume/realaudio/Radio_hoeren.html

Mannheim
Radio Regenbogen 102.8 MHz	Adult Contemp.	Click on the radio.	www.radio-regenbogen.de/real/index.htm

Munich
B5aktuell (Bayerischen Rund.)	News	Click on "LIVE!"	br.gmd.de/b5akt/b1.html
Bayern 3 (Bayerischer Rund.)	Variety	Click on the radio.	br.gmd.de/rv/bayern3/
HIT FM 89.0 MHz	Dance	"…very soon!"	www.hitfm.de/live.html

Stuttgart
SDR-1 (Süddeutscher Rund.)	News Bulletin	Click on "Nachrichten".	www.sdr.de/radio/sdr1/nachrichten/

Waldorf
Evangeliums Rundfunk (ERF 1)	Religion		www.erf.de/erf_live.htm
Evangeliums Rundfunk (ERF 2)	Contem. Christian		www.erf.de/erf_live.htm

GHANA—English

Accra
Joy FM 99.7 MHz	Hits		www.joy997fm.com.gh/broadcas.htm

GREECE—Greek

Athens
ERA 3 "102 FM"	Variety		www.ert3.gr/radio.htm
Flash 96.1 MHz	News/Pop		www.flash.gr/flash/flashlive.htm
KLIK FM 88.0 MHz	Pop		www.compulink.gr/klikfm/
Love Radio 99 FM	Love Songs		www.loveradio.gr/
Melodia FM 100	Rock/Greek Pop	Click the music-note circle.	www.melodia.gr/listen-index.html
Radio Gold 105.0 MHz	60's Rock		www.radiogold.gr/radiogold/home.htm
Spor FM 94.6 MHz	Sports/Greek Pop		www.sport.gr/sportfm.htm

Chania, Crete
MRB FM 101.0 MHz	Greek Pop	NetShow. IE4.0 required!	2m.grecian.net/greekradio/

Flórina
ERA Florinas 1278 kHz/96.6 MHz	Greek Pop	Not 24 hours. Inactive?	florina.compulink.gr/userpages/eraflori

Kalamata
HXW-FM 99.6 MHz	Call-Ins & Songs		klm.compulink.gr/hxw-fm/

Kavála			
StopFM 94.4 MHz	Greek Pop		www.kavala.hol.gr/body_en.htm
Lárisa			
Radio Palama 91.4 MHz	Variety		www.radiopalama.gr/
Orestiás			
ERA 4 Oriestiada	Variety	Click link at end of page.	www.evronet.gr/business/era4/index.htm
Radio Evros 97.1 MHz	Greek Pop		www.evronet.gr/business/revros/index.htm
Serres			
Radio One 101.0 MHz	Oldies/Dance		www.serres.hol.gr/media/radio1/
ERA 4 Serres	Variety		www.serres.hol.gr/media/era/
Thessaloníki			
Antenna FM "ANT1" 97.5 MHz	Popular Variety		www.ant1fm97-5.gr/real.htm
Cosmoradio 95.1 MHz	Greek Pop	Click on "RealAudio".	www.spark.net.gr/cosmoradio/
Radio 88 Miso 88.5 MHz	Rock		www.mylos.gr/88miso/
RadioXoros 101.6 MHz	Rock		www.radioxoros.gr/

GRENADA—English

St. George's			
Grenada Broadcasting Corporation 535 kHz/98.5	Variety/Urban	"Klassic 535 AM" shares time with "Sun FM".	www2.spiceisle.com/

GUAM—English

Agana			
KGUM 570 kHz	News Talk		www.radiopacific.com/k57/

GUATEMALA—Spanish

Guatemala City			
Emisoras Unidas 89.7 MHz	News/Sports	"5:00am-10:00pm"	www.centramerica.com/emisorasunidas/
Corporación Deportiva 93.1 MHz	Sports		www.starnet.net.gt/RCN/corpodep.htm

HAITI—Creole

Port-au-Prince			
Radio Vision 2000 99.3 MHz	Soft Rock	Live *via* Miami, Florida.	www.acn.com/

HOLLAND—Dutch

Amsterdam			
Radio 10 Gold 675 kHz	Classic Rock		www.radio10.nl/index2.html
Radio 100 98.3 MHz	Free Radio	Also **English**.	basis.desk.nl/~radio100/98-3f.htm
Radio Noord-Holland	Variety/News		www.nhkanaal.nl/welkom.html
VuurWerk	Dutch Rock	Click on "Klik hier".	www.radio.vuurwerk.nl/main.html
Bussum			
Radio 538 103.0 MHz	Pop		www.radio538.com/audio.html
Enschede			
Radio Enschede	Local Radio/Variety		www.twente.nl/media/radio/re/index.stm

Hilversum

De Concertzender	Classical/Mix		www.concertzender.nl/concertzender/ra/
NPS	Info & Culture		www.omroep.nl/nps/webradio/
Radio 3 FM	Rock		www.omroep.nl/radio3/
Radio Netherlands (RNW)	News & Features	Multilingual.	www.wrn.org/stations/rnw.html
Spoor 7	Contem. Christian	1-hour program.	www.omroep.nl/eo/spoor7/live/welcome.html
Veronica FM	Rock	Click on "RealAudio!"	www.veronica.nl/veronica/radio/
Veronica AM ("Music Highway")	Hits	Not 24 hours.	www.veronica.nl/musichighway/control/control.html

Naarden

Radio Noordzee Nationaal (RNN)	Pop		www.radio-noordzee.nl/live/index.html
SKY Radio 100.7 FM	Rock		www.skyradio.nl/

Rotterdam

Sun FM 104.9 MHz	Rock		www.sunfm.com/liveradio.html

The Hague

Arrow Classic Rock	Classic Rock	Click on "Luister".	www.arrow.nl/

HONDURAS—Spanish

Tegucigalpa

Power FM 89.3 MHz	LA Pop		www.globalnet.hn/powerfm/

HUNGARY—Hungarian

Budapest

Danubius Rádió 103.3 MHz	Rock	Click "On-line hallgatás".	www.danubius.hu/
Juventus Rádió 102.7 MHz	Rock	Click on the microphone.	www.juventus.hu/magyar/onlinehallgatas/onlinek.htm

Kossuth Rádió	Variety	Click loudspeaker icon.	www.kossuth.radio.hu/online.html
Petőfi Rádió	Pop	Click antenna tower icon.	www.petofi.radio.hu/reala.html
Rádió 1 100.3 MHz	Rock	Choose "R Di 1" in box.	www.datanet.hu/
Rádió Bridge 102.1 MHz	Rock	Click on "Hallgassa".	www.netropolisz.net/bridge/liv.htm
Radio Budapest	News/Music	**Multilingual.**	www.wrn.org/stations/hungary.html
ROXY Rádió 96.4 MHz	Rock	Not 24 hours.	www.hir.hu/roxy-maxy/
Star Rádió 92.9 MHz	Pop		www.star.irisz.hu/
Tilos Rádió 98.0 MHz	Jazz	Choose "Tilos R Di" in box. Not 24 hours.	www.datanet.hu/

Eger

Rádió Eger 101.3 MHz	Pop		www.agria.hu/radio/r_eger/live.html

Miskolc

City Rádió 96.3 MHz	Variety	Java problem? Click on the logo and choose "Open this file from its current location".	www.cityradio.hu/index2.htm

Siófok

Balaton Rádió 88.2 MHz	Rock & Pop		www.star.irisz.hu/

ICELAND—Icelandic

Reykjavik

Bylgjan	Rock	Click on "BYLGJAN".	www.frettir.is/media/
Kosmos Radio	Rock		www.xnet.is/
Radio X 97.7 MHz	Variety	Click on "X 977" logo.	www.xnet.is/xnet/margmidlun/radio/index.html
Ríkisútvarpi´ RUV	News Bulletin	Click on "Samantekt…"	this.is/ruv
RUV Rás 1	Variety	Click on logo. Not 24 hours but goes to Rás 2.	www.xnet.is/xnet/margmidlun/radio/ras1.html
RUV Rás 2	Eclectic	Click on "RAS2" logo.	www.xnet.is/ruv/
Útvarpsstö´in "FM957" 95.7 MHz	Rock	Click on "Í beinni í R.A."	xnet.is/fm957/

INDIA—English

Delhi

All India Radio	News, Music	Also **Hindi**. On demand *via* Flint, Michigan, USA.	air.kode.net/mc.htm
All India Radio: special internet program	Variety	Live audio. "Premium subscription charges.	air.kode.net/sch.htm

New Delhi

Corum Radio Asia	News & Music	Also **Hindi**.	www.radioasianet.com/program.html

INDONESIA—Indonesian

Bandung, Jawa
Ardan FM 105.8 MHz	**Rock**	0500-0800 UTC.	web.ardanfm.co.id/net-onair.html

Jakarta, Jawa
FMANIA 102.3 MHz	**Rock**		www.indosat.net.id/fm1023/

Medan, Sumatera
Prapanca FM 100.55 MHz	**Adult Contemp.**	Click "on air".	www.prapanca-fm.com/menu.htm
Radio KISS FM 104.75 MHz	**Rock**		www.kiss-fm.com/welcome.htm

IRAN—Farsi

Tehran
IRIB (Foreign-language Service)	**News & Info**	**Multilingual**.	www.irib.com/radio/boroonmarzi.htm
IRIB (Persian Service)	**Variety**	Direct URL:	www.irib.com/radio/real/radio1.ram
Islamic Rep. of Iran Broadcasting	**News**	On demand bulletins.	www.irna.com/radio.html
Islamic Rep. of Iran Broadcasting	**News**	Relayed from shortwave.	www.netiran.com/Frame-Html/DailyNews/irib.html

IRELAND—English

Casla
Raidió na Gaeltachta	**Talk Features**	**Irish Gaelic**. Inactive?	rnag.wombat.ie/rnag/fuaim.html

Dublin
RTE 2FM	**Pop/Variety**		www.2fm.ie/tunein/
RTE Radio One	**News & Features**	Also **Irish Gaelic**.	www.rte.ie/radio/radioone.html
RTE Dublin Ireland	**News**	Also **Irish Gaelic**.	www.wrn.org/stations/rte.html

Waterford
ABC Power 104 104.1 MHz	**Hits**		homepages.iol.ie/~abcpower/

ISRAEL—Hebrew

Jerusalem
Galey Tzh'hal	**News Headlines**		www.glz.co.il/~ofer/Hebrew/News/newest.html
Golshim Bareshet	**Sample Program**		www.90fm.co.il/
Israel Club	**Media samples**		www.artificia.com/html/news/newsexam.cgi
Kol Israel	**News**	**English**. On demand.	www.virtual.co.il/city_services/news/kolra.htm
Kol Israel "Radio Shalom"	**News Bulletin**	**French**. On demand.	www.cyberj.com/info/index.html
Radio 10 106.7 MHz	**"Positive Jewish"**		www.radio10.co.il/
Reshet Bet (Israel Radio)	**News**		bet.netvision.net.il/

Sharon
Radios (Radius) 100FM	**Israeli Pop**		www.100fm.co.il/ra/

> Italian songs have come a long way from *Volare*. Fall in love again by listening to Florence's own Radio Fiesole, which airs nothing but Italian *musica bella*.
> R. Fiesole

Tel Aviv

Arutz-7 1143 kHz/105.2 MHz	Religion	English, some evenings.	www.a7.org/live.htm
Radio Tel Aviv 102.0 MHz	Rock		www.102fm.co.il/live/

ITALY—Italian

Bari
L'AltraRadio 93.1 MHz	Italian Pop		www.pangeanet.it/laltraradio/

Bergamo
Radio Alta 101.7 MHz	Rock		www2.spm.it/Radio/

Bologna
Radio Italia Network	Italian Rock	Click on "Ascolta".	www.italianetwork.it/prehome.htm

Bolzano
RAI TGR Network	Regional News	German.	www.tin.it/tgr/temp/grbolzanolt.htm

Cesena
Radio Studio Delta 92.8 MHz	Rock	Click on "Go".	www.radiostudiodelta.it/realaudio.htm

Cuneo
Radio Stereo 5 100.6 MHz	News/Features	On demand site.	www.multiwire.net/ra/realaudio.html

Diano Marina/Imperia
RCB Radio Capoberta FM	Italian Pop		gnews.it/rcb/index.htm

Firenze
Radio Fiesole 100	Italian Music	Off-air audio problems.	www.fiesole100.it/

Locri
Radio DJ Club Studio 54	Italian Pop		www.radioitalia.net/

Matera
Radio Anch'io	Italian Pop	Click on "diretta su Internet!!!". Not 24 hours.	www.hsh.it/anchio/index.htm

Milan
Radio 101	Rock	Start NetShow player.	www.radio101.it/netshow/
Radio Peter Flowers FM	Rock/Techno	Direct URL:	www.tiesseci.it/tscshop3/pf.ram
Radio Planet FM	Rock	Click on the logo.	www.radioplanet.it/

RockFM 98.7 MHz	Rock	Click on "Ascoltaci".	www.radiorockfm.com/realaudio/ra_conten.html
Napoli			
Radio Marte 95.6/97.7 MHz	Talk Radio/Pop	Not 24 hours.	www.radiomarte.it/ONAIR/
Padova			
Radio Padova 103.9 MHz	Rock		intercity.shiny.it/radiopd/rpdlive.html
Rome			
Radio Dimensione Suono	Popular Variety		www.rds.it/radio/real/index.htm
Radio Emme 100 100.0 MHz	Dance/Techno		m100.micanet.it/
Radio L'Olgiata 96.6 MHz	Italian Pop	NetShow.	www.ilink.it/radioolgiata/
Radio Radio 104.5 MHz	Talk Radio	Click on "Radio in Diretta".	www.radioradio.it/
RAI TGR Network	Regional News	Local news from all Italy.	www.tin.it/tgr/temp/nostrigr.htm
RAI TGR Network "Italia in diretta"	National News		www.tin.it/tgr/rubriche/italiain.htm
RTL 102.5 MHz	Hits	Select "LIVE RADIO".	net.gnews.it/net/guest/rtl/
Trieste			
RAI TGR Network	Pop	Slovene.	www.tin.it/tgr/temp/grtriestels.htm
Vicenza			
Radio Vicenza 103.2 MHz	Rock		www.radiovicenza.it/html/info.htm

JAMAICA—English

Kingston

Radio Jamaica Limited	Sports/Reggae	On demand site.	www.radiojamaica.com/

JAPAN—Japanese

Hayama

Shibuya-FM 78.4 MHz	Progressive	Live. Click on "TUNE".	www.parco-city.co.jp/shibuya-fm/
Shibuya-FM 78.4 MHz	Variety	Programs on demand.	www.parco-city.co.jp/shibuya-fm/ondemand.html
Shonan BeachFM 78.9 MHz	Jazz/Eclectic	Live and on demand.	www.beachfm.co.jp/

Shonan

Fantastic Radio Station	Program Samples		jpx.com/

Takamatsu

FM Takamatsu "Mandegan" 81.5 MHz	Variety	Click on the small satellite dish. Not 24 hours. ISDN?	www.pasutel.co.jp/onair/top.htm

Tokyo

Music Bird Internet Radio	Variety	Click "SOUND ON".	www.tfm.co.jp/MB/
Radio Tampa	Reports		www.tampa.co.jp/dial/report.html

JORDAN—English

Amman

JRTV (Radio Jordan)	Interviews	Download files.	www.jrtv.com/

KENYA—English

Nairobi

Kenya Broadcasting Corp. (KBC)	News	Also **Swahili**.	www.africaonline.co.ke/AfricaOnline/netradio.html

KOREA (REPUBLIC)—Korean

Seoul

KBS 1 711 kHz/97.3 MHz	News & Info		kbsnt.kbs.co.kr/
KBS 2 89.1 MHz	Korean Pop		kbsnt.kbs.co.kr/
MBC 900 kHz/95.9 MHz	Variety	Click on "AM", top-right.	radio.mbc.co.kr/
MBC 91.9 MHz	Pop	Click on "FM", top-right.	radio.mbc.co.kr/
PSB "Blue Wave" 99.9 MHz	Variety/Pop	Click on "FM Radio".	www.psb.co.kr/FM/
Radio Korea International	News & Info	**Multilingual.** Live and on demand news.	210.115.193.23/
Radio Korea International	News & Info	**Multilingual.**	kbsnt.kbs.co.kr/rki/rki.html
SBS 792 kHz	Korean Pop	Click on loudspeaker.	ps.sbswebvision.com/radio/radio_f.html
SBS "Power FM" 107.7 MHz	Korean Pop	Click on loudspeaker.	ps.sbswebvision.com/fm/fm_f.html
TBC "Dream FM" 99.3 MHz	Lite Rock	Click the top-right blue button, over "Realplay".	www.tbc.co.kr/atfm/main0.html
Yonhap Television News (YTN)	News Channel	Click "Video + Audio via Streamworks."	www.ytn.co.kr/ytn10.htm

KUWAIT—Arabic

Kuwait City

Radio Kuwait	News	On demand site.	www.radiokuwait.org/

LATVIA—Latvian

Riga

Latvijas Radio	News Bulletins	Also **English**, **Russian**.	www.radio.org.lv/realaud/LR_AUDIO.HTM

LEBANON—Arabic

Beirut
Radio One FM 105.5 MHz	**Adult Contemp.**	English.	www.radioone.com.lb/radio1/main.htm

Jounieh
The Voice of Charity Radio	**Catholic**	Sometimes in **English**.	www.radiocharity.org.lb/main.html

LIECHTENSTEIN—German

Triesen
Radio L (and occasionally others)	**News Bulletins**	On demand site.	www.lol.li/

LITHUANIA—Lithuanian

Vilnius
Lietuvos Radijo Radio 1	**Variety**	Click Transliacija Internete.	www.lrtv.lt/
M-1 Plius	**Variety**	Not 24 hours.	www.m-1.lt/nnintrnet/M1PLIUS/Default.html
Radijo Stotis M-1	**Top 40**		www.m-1.lt/nnintrnet/M1/Default.html

LUXEMBOURG—Luxembourgian

Luxembourg
Eldoradio 105.0/107.2 MHz	**Rock**		www.eldoradio.lu/livestream/

MACEDONIA—Macedonian

Ohrid
Radio Ohrid 89.0/98.8 MHz	**Daily News**	On demand.	www.soros.org.mk/radioohrid/

Skopje
MRT Macedonian Radio (Skopje)	**Local Music/Variety**		www.unet.com.mk/mrt/live.htm

MALAYSIA—Malaysian

Kuala Lumpur
RTM	**Variety**	**Multilingual**. Six programs but server is overloaded.	www.asiaconnect.com.my/rtm-net/live/
Time Highway Radio 99.3 MHz	**Pop/Rock**	**English**. Inactive?	thr.time.com.my/

MEXICO—Spanish

Acapulco
Cerebro FM (XHGRC) 97.7MHz	**Rock/Eclectic**	NetShow. Not 24 hrs.	www.acaweb.com/cerebro/sched1.htm

Chihuahua
El Lobo (XHSU) 106.1 MHz	**Rock**		www.online.com.mx/ellobo/106/

Ciudad Victoria
R. Universidad (XHUNI) 102.5	**Latina**		www.uat.mx/Difusion/radio/

Guadalajara
Super Stereo "la radio pirata"	**Rock**	Univ. de Guadalajara.	www.superstereo.com.mx/
R. Universidad (XHUG) 104.3	**Variety**	Univ. de Guadalajara.	server.radio.udg.mx/

Mérida
R. Universidad (XERUY) 103.9	Variety	U. Autónoma de Yucatán.	www.uady.mx/~ruady/rauady.html

Mexicali
Radio Cetys	College Radio	Cetys Univ. Not 24 hrs.	www.mxl.cetys.mx/radiocetys/

Mexico City
"WFM" (XEW) 96.9 MHz	Rock		www.wfm.com.mx/mfw/index.html
Alfa (XHRCA) 91.3 MHz	Dance		radiocentro.com.mx/alfa91.3/
El Fonógrafo (XERC) 790 kHz	Nostalgia	Click on "Live Audio".	radiocentro.com.mx/elfonografo/
Formato 21 (XECMQ) 1150 kHz	News/Reports		canal.grc.com.mx/ie4/hoy/default.htm
La Z (XHFO) 92.1 MHz	Groups		radiocentro.com.mx/laz/
R. Consentida (XEFAJ) 1560 kHz	Ranchera	Click on "Escúchenos".	radiocentro.com.mx/consentida/
R. Variedades (XERTM) 1320 kHz	LA Groups		radiocentro.com.mx/variedades/
Radio Centro (XEQR) 1030 kHz	Romantic Ballads		radiocentro.com.mx/rcentro/
Radio RED (XERED) 1110 kHz	News/Talk Radio		radiocentro.com.mx/red/
Radio RED (XHRED) 88.1 MHz	Pop Variety	Click on "Escúchenos".	radiocentro.com.mx/redfm88.1/
Radio UNAM (XEUN) 860 kHz	News & Info	Select right "Sintonizar". 7:00-1:00 local time.	serpiente.dgsca.unam.mx/radiounam/
R. UNAM (XEUN-FM) 96.1 MHz	Cultural/News	Select left "Sintonizar". Univ. Nacional Autónoma.	serpiente.dgsca.unam.mx/radiounam/
Stereo 97.7 (XERC-FM)	"Música Moderna"		radiocentro.com.mx/97.7/ie40/default.html
Stereo Joya (XEJP-FM) 93.7 MHz	Pop		radiocentro.com.mx/joya93.7/
Universal Stereo (XEQR-FM) 107.3	Rock	Click on the red button.	radiocentro.com.mx/universal107.3/
VOX FM (XEX-FM) 101.7 MHz	Variety		www.voxfm.com/mexico/REAL/realaudio.html

Monterrey
D99 (XHJD) 98.9 MHz	?	Future Plans.	www.intercable.net/d99/
TU 1/2	Eclectic/Rock		tumedio.mty.itesm.mx/

Piedras Negras
La Rancherita (XEMU) 580 kHz	Ranchera		www.la-rancherita.com.mx/

Puebla
SICOM FM (XHSIC) 105.9 MHz	Educational	8:00-16:00 local time.	www.sicomnet.edu.mx/sicom/HTML/SI_Hfm.htm

Queretaro
Mix FM 97.9 MHz	Rock		queretaro.infosel.com.mx/Acir.html

Tijuana
Radio Latina (XLTN) 104.5 MHz	Latina Pop		www.radiolatina.com/latinalive.htm
X99 (XHKY) 99.3 MHz	Ranchera		www.x99.com/index2.htm

MOLDOVA—Moldavian

Chisinau
Radio Nova 105.9 MHz	Musical Requests	One live hour per day.	www.novaradio.com/realaud.html

MONACO—English

Monte Carlo
Riviera Radio 106.3 MHz	Interviews	On demand site.	www.riviera-radio.com/liveaud.htm

MOROCCO—Arabic

Rabat

RTV Marocaine "R. Casablanca"	**Indigenous Music**	ShockWave+RA.	www.maroc.net/rc/boite.html
RTV Marocaine "R. Casablanca"	**News**	Multilingual.	www.maroc.net/rc/actualites.htm

Tanger

MEDI 1 R. Méditerranée Internat.	**News/Info/Music**	Also in **French**. 0500-0100 UTC.	www.medi1.com/medi1/radio.htm

NEPAL—Nepali

Kathmandu

Radio Nepal	**News/Songs**	Also **English**.	www.catmando.com/news/radio-nepal/

NETHERLANDS ANTILLES—Papiamento

Curaçao

Radio Korsou 93.9 MHz	**Antillean Pop**	Also **Dutch**.	www.korsou.com/live/

NEW ZEALAND—English

Auckland

"95bFM" 95.0 MHz	**Freeform**	Auckland University.	www.95bfm.co.nz/cool.html
More FM 91.8 MHz	**Rock**		www.91.8fm.co.nz/listen.html

Wellington

91 ZM "Zed M"	**Alternative**		www.audionet.co.nz/live.html
Channel Z 94.7/98.5 MHz	**Rock**		www.channelz.co.nz/listen.html
Radio Active 89FM	**Diverse**		www.radioactive.co.nz/real.html
More FM 98.9 MHz	**Today's Best**		www.morefm.com/
NewsTalk ZB 1035kHz	**Rugby**	Hurricanes games.	www.hurricanes.co.nz/times.html
R. New Zealand National Station	**Variety**	Select "Live-National".	www.rnz.co.nz/index30.html
R. New Zealand International	**News About N.Z.**	On demand site.	www.wrn.org/stations/rnzi.html
R. New Zealand International	**Pacific News**	On demand site.	www.audionet.co.nz/ranz.html

NICARAGUA—Spanish

Managua

Radio Corporación 540 kHz	**Editorials**	On demand site.	www.rc540.com.ni/programacion.htm

NORWAY—Norwegian

Oslo

Democratic Voice of Burma	**News**	**Burmese**. On demand.	www.communique.no/dvb/programs/
NRK Alltid Nyheter	**All News**	Click "Hør Alltid Nyheter som". Carries BBC World Service in English, 21:05-06:00, Oslo local time.	www.nrk.no/alltidnyheter/
NRK Radio 1	**Headlines**	On demand.	www.nrk.no/radionyheter/dagsnytt/ra.html
P4 Radio Hele Norge	**Hourly News**		www.p4.no/nyheter/p4lyd/

P4 Radio Hele Norge	Rock	Click "P4s livesending".	www.p4.no/live/
Radio 1 102.0 MHz	Variety		www.sn.no/radio1/reala.src.html
Radio Tango 99.3 MHz	Music	Click on "LIVE".	www.riksnett.no/radiotango/
Voice of Tibet	News	**Tibetan.** On demand.	www.vot.org/
Trondheim			
Akademisk Radioklubb - LA1K	Student Radio	During October-November "UKA" festival.	www.uka.ntnu.no/gjenger/kultur/ukesender/uslive.html

OMAN—Arabic

Muscat

Sultanate of Oman Radio & TV	Mideast Variety	0200-2130 UTC.	www.oman-tv.gov.om/

PAKISTAN—English

Islamabad

Pakistan Broadcasting Corporation	News	Also **Urdu**. Requires "VoxWare" software.	radio.gov.pk/
Radio Pakistan	News		members.aol.com/nvalliani/index.html

Karachi

FM100	Songs	On demand site.	www.fm100pak.com/index.htm

PANAMA—Spanish

David

Radio Chiriquí (HOB55) 780 kHz	News/Info/Sports		www.chiriqui.com/radiochiriqui/

Panama City

Continental Estéreo	Rock		www.sinfo.net/sinfomusic/em8.html
Estéreo Bahía 105.7 MHz	Smooth Pop		www.sinfo.net/sinfomusic/em5.html
La Exitosa 930 kHz/95.3 MHz	Rhythmic/Sports		www.sinfo.net/exitosa/

Announcer Osvaldo Amilkar (striped shirt), Argentinian model Daniela Cardone, Tony Apuril of the satirical group "Ab Ovo," and announcer Leticia Medina relax after a Saturday comedy show at Paraguayan FM station Canal 100.
Canal Cien

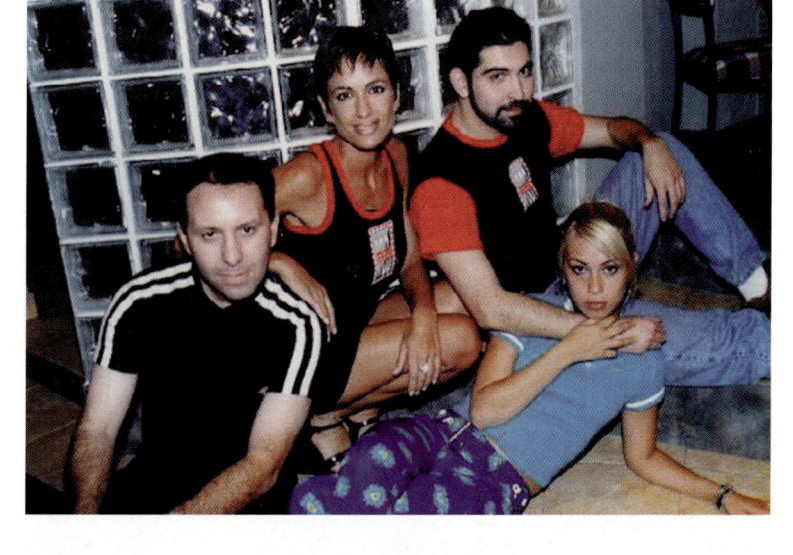

Omega Stereo 107.3 MHz	Rock	Click on "omega.sinfo.net".	omega.sinfo.net/
Patatus 93.9 MHz	Caribe		www.sinfo.net/sinfomusic/em10.html
Radio 10 88.1 MHz	Rock		www.radio10.com/
Radio Mia 96.7 MHz	News Talk/Sports		www.radiomia.com/bienvenida.html
Radio Mix 97.9 MHz	Variety		www.sinfo.net/sinfomusic/em7.html
KW Continente 700 kHz	Variety	Click on "Radio Reloj".	www.elsiglo.com/principal.html
Stereo Panamá 106.7 MHz	Hits	Not 24 hours.	www.sinfo.net/sinfomusic/em9.html
Super Q 90.5 MHz	Tropical		www.sinfo.net/sinfomusic/em14.html
Tropical Moon 88.9 MHz	Tropical Jazz		www.tropimoon.com/

PAPUA NEW GUINEA—English

Port Moresby

Nau FM 96.5 MHz	Variety	Click on "GO!"	www.naufm.com.pg/tunein.htm

PARAGUAY—Spanish

Asunción

Radio Canal 100 100.1 MHz	Pop	Click on the logo box.	www.canal100.com.py/main.htm
Radio Cardinal 730 kHz	News & Sports		www.infonet.com.py/NoticiasOnLine/
Radio —andutí AM 1020 kHz	News Talk	Click on the microphone.	www.nanduti.com.py/
Radio —andutí AM 1020 kHz	News Talk	Click on the logo.	www.infonet.com.py/holding1/
Radio —andutí FM 107.7 MHz	Folklórica	On demand site.	www.infonet.com.py/holding/nandufm/musica.htm
Radio Venus 105.1 MHz	Rock & Pop		www.venus.com.py/html/front.html
Rock & Pop 95.5 MHz	Rock & Pop		www.rockandpop.com.py/

Pedro Juan Caballero

Amambay FM 100.5 MHz	Pop	Audio may be suspended.	server.pontapora.com.br/~amambay/

PERU—Spanish

Lima

Radioprogramas del Perú 730 kHz	News	Click on the microphone.	www.rpp.com.pe/indexa2.ssi

PHILIPPINES—Tagalog

Manila

DWRR 101.9 MHz dwrrlive.html	Soft Rock	English.	www.abs-cbn.com/entertainment/radshows/
DZMM 630 kHz	Pop		www.abs-cbn.com/entertainment/radshows/dzmm/dzmmlive/
Far East Broadcasting Company	Sample Clips	Multilingual. Requires iWave.	www.febc.org/music.html

POLAND—Polish

Cracow

R. Akademickie Kraków 100.5 MHz	Eclectic	Click on "STEREO".	ituner.com/rak/
Radio Muzyka Fakty (RMF)	Rock		realaudio.rmf.pl/

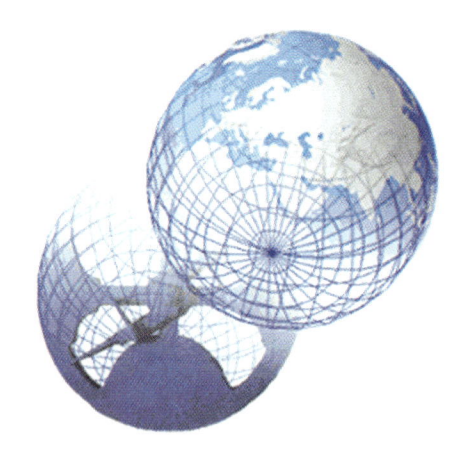

Jelenia
Radio Jowisz   **Pop**   www.jowisz.pl/raudio.html

Katowice
Radio Flash FM 72.2/106.4 MHz   **Rock/News**   www.flash.com.pl/index.htm

Slupsk
Radio City 66.5 MHz/100.9 MHz   **Rock**   www.city.ct.com.pl/RealAudioPage.htm

Szczecin
Radio AS 65.96/88.9 MHz   **Polish Pop**   Plays automatically.   www.dragon.com.pl/radio_as.htm

Warsaw
Polish Radio Warsaw   **News & Info**   Also **English**.   www.wrn.org/stations/poland.html
Polskie Radio 1   **Variety**   www.radio.com.pl/jedynka/
Polskie Radio 3   **News & Info**   www.radio.com.pl/trojka/realaudio/

Wroclaw
Radio Eska 104.9 MHz   **Rock**   www.eska.com.pl/
Radio Klakson 106.1 MHz   **Entertainment**   Program Samples.   www.wroclaw.com/klakson2.htm

PORTUGAL—Portuguese

Aveiro
Rádio Moliceiro 94.4 MHz   **Pop**   NetShow.   www.ciberguia.pt/radiomoliceiro/

Lisbon
Rádio Comercial   **Pop**   Click the play button.   www.radiocomercial.pt/Audio/f_emissao.html
RDP - Radiodifusão   **All formats**   Live audio in   www.rdp.pt/
Portuguesa   development.
Super FM 95.3 MHz   **Variety**   Poor off-air sound.   www.superfm.com/
TSF Rádio Notícias 89.5MHz   **News**   www.tsf.pt/tsf.html

PUERTO RICO—Spanish

Guayama
WMEG "La Mega Estación"   **Rock**   StreamWorks.   www.megaestacion.com/vivo.htm
106.9

San Juan
Cadena NCN   **Religion**   StreamWorks.   ncn.coqui.net/radio.html

WIAC "Sistema 102" 102.5 MHz	Pop		www.sistema102.com/
WIPR "Allegro" 91.3 MHz	Classical	StreamWorks.	wipr.coqui.net/radio.htm
WIPR-AM 940 kHz	News & Info	StreamWorks.	wipr.coqui.net/radio.htm
WPRM Cadena Sal Soul 98.5	Salsa	Click the ball. Poor audio.	www.salsoulaudio.com/
WSKN "La Súper Kadena" 630	News		www.spiderlink.net/superkadena/

REUNION—French

St. Denis

NRJ REUNION	Rock	Click "RA NRJ" logo.	www.guetali.fr/nrj/etage1/default.htm
RFO Réunion	News Bulletins		www.rfo.fr/html/info/bulletins.html

ROMANIA—Romanian

Brasov

Pro FM 70.1 MHz	Rock	Not 24 hours.	profm.deltanet.roknet.ro/
Radio Brasov 87.8 MHz	News/Hits	Under development.	www.deuroconsult.ro/rbv/

Bucharest

PRO FM 102.8 MHz	Rock	Poor audio quality.	www.profm.ro/real.htm
R. România Actualitati (Program 1)	Variety		www.ituner.com/rom.htm

Craiova

Radio Horion 103.6 MHz	Hits		www.cisnet.ro/horion/
Radio Sud 97.4 MHz	Rock		www.cisnet.ro/radiosud/

Iasi

Radio Hit 94.9 MHz	Rock		radiohit.dntis.ro/live.html

Târgu Mures

Radio Contact 90.2 MHz	Rock		www.ituner.com/netsoft/contact.html
Radio Uniplus 72.68 MHz	Rock		www.ituner.com/netsoft/uniplus.html

Timisoara

Radio Europa Nova 89.7 MHz	Rock	Click on left microphone.	www.novatm.ro/
Radio Vest 88.7 MHz	Variety		www.radiovest.ro/

RUSSIA—Russian

Chelyabinsk

Studio 1 71.96 MHz	Variety	Select day(s) of week. Not 24 hours. StreamWorks.	www.urc.ac.ru/SW/

Ekaterinburg

Radio C 68.39 MHz/103.7 MHz	Rock & Pop		www.radioc.ru/onair.htm

Moscow

Echo of Moscow 73.82/91.0 MHz	News/Talk Radio	Click small loudspeaker.	www.echo.msk.ru/real_audio.htm
Radio 101 1233 kHz/ 101.2 MHz	Music Selections	On demand site.	www.101.ru/hit101.htm
Radio Silver Rain 100.1 MHz	Pop		www.sr.ru/s1.htm
Russkoe Radio 105.7 MHz	Hits		www.russianet.ru/rusradio/eindex.html
Voice of Russia	News	Also **English**.	www.wrn.org/stations/vor.html

Russkoe Radio's Gleb Deyev (top), Anna Maslova (left) and Maria Sergeyeva (right).

St. Petersburg
Radio Modern 72.14/ 104.0 MHz — Dance — www.modern.dux.ru/index_e.html

Samara
Samara-Maximum 104.3 MHz — Variety — www.max.samara.ru/

Togliatty
August Radio 102.3 MHz — Rock — Click "RealAudio" logo. www.august.ru/AugustRADIO/start.htm

Vladivostok
Radio VBC 612 kHz / 101.7 MHz — Rock — www.primorye.ru/Radio/VBC/

SENEGAL—French

Dakar

Radio Nostalgie Dakar 90.3 MHz	**West African Pop**	Technical problems.	www.metissacana.sn/nostalgie/
RTV Sénégalaise	**Variety**	NetShow. Click "Ecoutez la Radio". Not 24 hours.	www.primature.sn/rts/prog.htm
Sud FM 98.5 MHz	**Variety**	Technical problems.	www.metissacana.sn/sud/sudfm.html
Walf-FM	**West African Pop**	Click on "WALF-FM" box.	www1.telecomplus.sn/walf/

SINGAPORE—Chinese

Singapore

Radio Corporation of Singapore	**All Formats**	Multilingual.	rcslive.singnet.com.sg/
Radio Singapore International	**News/Features**	Also **English/Malay**.	www.rsi.com.sg/current.htm
RCS "Class 95 FM" 95.0 MHz	**Adult Contemp.**	English.	www.rcs.com.sg/class95/
RCS "One FM" 90.5 MHz	**"Infotainment"**	English.	www.rcs.com.sg/onefm/
RCS "Symphony 92.4" 92.4 MHz	**Classical/Jazz**	English.	www.rcs.com.sg/924/
RCS "Perfect 10" 98.7 MHz	**Contemp. Hit**	English.	www.rcs.com.sg/p10/
RCS "Capital Radio" 95.8 MHz	**"Infotainment"**		www.rcs.com.sg/958/
RCS "FM 93.3" 93.3 MHz	**Contemp. Hit**		www.rcs.com.sg/933/
RCS "Love" 97.2 MHz	**Pop**		www.rcs.com.sg/972/index1.html
RCS "Ria" 89.7 MHz	**News Talk/Pop**	Malay.	www.rcs.com.sg/ria/html/about.htm
RCS "Warna" 94.2 MHz	**Comtem. Hit**	Malay.	www.rcs.com.sg/warna/wmenu.htm
RCS "Oli" 96.8 MHz	**Music & Info**	Tamil.	www.rcs.com.sg/oli/
SAFRA Radio "Dong Li" 88.3 MHz	**Chinese Pop**	Click on "DL Live". StreamWorks.	fm883.com.sg/

SLOVAKIA—Slovak

Bratislava

Radio Twist 101.8 MHz	**Pop**	Twelve 15-minute clips.	realaudio.eunet.sk/twist/live/live.html

SLOVENIA—Slovene

Ljubljana

Radio Ognjišèe	**Catholic/Pop**		www.ognjisce.si/ognjisce/iradio/
Radio Slovenija	**Variety/Classical**	First two pages click ear, third page click desired music note.	www.rtvslo.si/radio/indexi.html

SOUTH AFRICA—English

Bloemfontein

Radio Hoogland	**Variety**	Afrikaans.	studbook.co.za/hoogland/

Johannesburg

Channel Africa	**Reports/Features**	Multilingual.	www.sabc.co.za/units/chanafr/ra/index.html
Channel Africa	**News**	On demand bulletin.	www.wrn.org/stations/africa.html
Impact Radio 103 FM	**Christian**		www.impact-radio.co.za/index2.htm
SABC "5FM"	**Rock**		www.5fm.co.za/

SABC "Kaya FM" 95.9 MHz	Adult Contemp.	Not always working.	www.avnet.co.za/avhome1.htm
SABC "Metro FM"	African Pop		www.qradio.net/
SABC "SA FM"	News Talk	"Live Test Broadcasting".	www.avnet.co.za/avhome1.htm
SABC "SA FM"	News Bulletin	On demand broadcast.	www.qradio.net/
SABC "Ukhozi FM"	Variety	Zulu.	www.qradio.net/

SPAIN—Spanish

Barcelona

Catalunya Informació	News	Catalan.	www.catradio.es/cr/cr-direc.html
Catalunya Música	Classical	Catalan.	www.catradio.es/cr/cr-direc.html
Catalunya Ràdio	Variety	Catalan.	www.catradio.es/cr/cr-direc.html
COMRàdio	News Talk	Catalan.	com-radio.com/directe.htm
Els matins amb Josep Cuní	News/Features	Catalan. On demand.	www.partal.com/cuni/
RAC 105	Pop Variety	Catalan.	www.catradio.es/cr/cr-direc.html

Girona

Enteranyinats	Interviews	Catalan. On demand.	www.girona.intercom.es/enteranyinats/arxiura.html

Lleida

Segre Ràdio 93.4 MHz	Hits	Catalan.	www.segreradio.com/

Madrid

Cadena COPE	News Talk		www.cope.es/
Cadena SER	News/Talk/Sports	Click on "En el Aire".	www.cadenaser.es/scripts/cadenaser/cserprt.asp
Onda Cero Radio 98.0 MHz	Talk	Click the "ON" button.	ondacero.adam.es/index_0.htm
Onda Madrid 1 101.3/106.0 MHz	News/Pop/Sports	Click on the headphones.	www.telemadrid.com/ondamadrid/
Radio Exterior de España	News & Features		www.rtve.es/rne/ree/index.htm

Santiago de Compostela

Radio Galega	Variety		www.crtvg.es/RadioDirecta/RadioDirecto.html

Seville

Canal Sur Radio	News & Info		www.canalsur.es/dir.html

SRI LANKA—English

Colombo

Sirasa FM 106.5 MHz	Variety	Sinhala.	www.mega.lk/sirasafm/listen.htm
TNL Radio 90.0/101.7 MHz	Variety	0600-2400 Sri Lanka Time.	www.lanka.net/comdex/asialive/tnl.html

SURINAME—Sranang Tongo

Paramaribo

Radio ABC	News	On demand site.	www.parbo.com/dwt/

SWEDEN—Swedish

Borås

Radio Match 105.5 MHz	Rock		www.radiomatch.se/instruktionerradio.html

Lund

Radio AF 99.1 MHz	College Radio	Akademiska Föreningen.	www.af.lu.se/af/radioaf/

VOICES FROM HOME 79

Stockholm

Bandit 105.5	New Rock		www.bandit.se/live/index.html
Power Hit Radio	Hits	StreamWorks.	www.power106.com/
Radio City 105.9 MHz	Rock	Requires ISDN.	www.power106.com/
Radio Sweden	News	On demand daily.	www.sr.se/rs/svenska/ny3.htm
Radio Sweden	News & Info	Multilingual.	www.sr.se/rs/realaudi.htm
Sveriges Radio	Variety	On demand library.	www.sr.se/lyssna/
Sveriges Radio Ekot	News/Archives	On demand clips.	www.sr.se/ekot/
Vinyl 107 107.1 MHz	60's Songs	StreamWorks.	www.vinyl107.se/live.html

Umeå

Radio RIX 104.2 MHz	Rock		www.rix.se/

Växjö

Hit FM 105.8 MHz	Rock/Pop		www.hitfm.se/hitfm2.htm

SWITZERLAND—German

Basel

Radio Basilisk	Hits		www.basilisk.ch/

Bern

Schweizer Radio DRS 3	Features		web.eunet.ch/drs3/drdaud01.htm

Brugg				
Radio Argovia 90.3/ 94.0 MHz	Variety/Rock		www.winet.ch/argovia/haupt.html	
Buchs				
Radio Ri	Headlines	On demand news.	www.rol.ch/BuchsMedien/Radio/audio.htm	
Chur				
Radio Grischa	Eclectic	Click on the globe.	www.radiogrischa.ch/home/onair.htm	
Fribourg				
Radio Fribourg 89.4 MHz	Rock	French. NetShow.	www.radiofr.ch/	
Interlaken				
Radio BeO (Berner Oberland)	Pop/Variety		www.beo-radio.ch/	
Lausanne				
Espace 2 (R. Suisse Romande)	News/Features	French. On demand.	www.espace2.ch/	
La Première (R. Suisse Romande)	News/Features	French. On demand.	http://www.lapremiere.ch/	
R. Couleur 3 (R. Suisse Romande)	Hip-Hop/Techno	French. In construction.	www.couleur3.ch/	
Lucerne				
Radio Pilatus 95.8/104.9 MHz	News/Reports		www.radio-pilatus.ch/week/week.htm	
Lugano				
RTSI Rete 2	Discussions	Italian.	www.rtsi.ch/rete2/osserva/osserva.htm	
Rapperswil				
Radio Zürisee	Classic Rock	Direct URL: www. radio.ch/ramfile/live.ram	www.radio.ch/ONAIR/Onair.htm	
Rotkreuz				
Radio Sunshine 88	Pop Variety		www.sunshine.ch/	
St. Gallen				
Radio Aktuel 92.9/88.0 MHz	Pop Variety		www.radioaktuell.ch/	
Zürich				
Radio 24 102.8 MHz	Hits & News	Rock.	radio24.eunet.ch/	
Radio Z 100.9 MHz	Hits & News		radioz.unit.net/	

TANZANIA—Swahili

Dar Es Salaam

Radio One	Variety	Also **English**.	www.ippmedia.com/Newspapers/radio1.asp

THAILAND—Thai

Bangkok

Army Television/TV5—FM 94.0	Pop	Click on "listen".	www.tv5.co.th/
Business Radio 96.5 MHz	Business News	NetShow.	www.thaicast.ksc.net/inn/inn_fm96.html
FM 97 "Trinity Radio" 97.0	News/Music	NetShow.	www.thaicast.ksc.net/fm97/
Green Wave 104.5 MHz	Thai Pop	Click on "Green Wave".	www.intercast.loxinfo.co.th/index.html
Hotwave 91.5 MHz	Variety	Click on "Hotwave".	www.intercast.loxinfo.co.th/index.html
Love FM 94.5 MHz	Love Songs	NetShow.	www.thaicast.ksc.net/bnt/love94.htm
Nation Radio 90.5 MHz	Variety		www.intercast.loxinfo.co.th/nation/html/nation.html
Radio No Problem 88.0 MHz	Thai Pop	Click "Radio No Problem".	www.intercast.loxinfo.co.th/index.html
Radio Vote Satelite 93.5 MHz	Thai Pop	Click "Radio Vote Satelite".	www.intercast.loxinfo.co.th/index.html
Siam Sport Radio 99.0 MHz	Sports/Talk		www.intercast.loxinfo.co.th/sradio/html/index.html
TIS "Radio Thailand" 92.5 MHz	News	Click "925 MHz LIVE".	207.96.8.147/radio/

Hat Yai

Magic Radio 104.0 MHz	Pop Variety		www.escati.com/magic_radio.htm

Nakhon Ratchasima

Suranaree University of Tech.	Public Affairs	Live and on demand.	sut2.sut.ac.th/sut2/

TUNISIA—Arabic

Tunis

Radio Tunis (Tunisia National Radio)	Variety		www.radiotunis.com/live.html

TURKEY—Turkish

Ankara

Capital Radio 99.5 MHz	Top 40		www.capitalradio.com.tr/

Istanbul

Akra FM 107.6 MHz	Traditional	Click "CANLI YAYIN".	www.akra.com.tr/anasayfa.htm
ITU RADYO 103.8 MHz	Classical	Click "ITU RADYO LIVE".	www.ehb.itu.edu.tr/~ituradyo/
ITU RADYO 103.8 MHz	Classical	Alternate URL:	radyo.ehb.itu.edu.tr/
Kent FM 101.1 MHz	Rock		www.kentfm.com.tr/
Power FM 100.0 MHz	Variety		www.powerfm.com.tr/live.htm
Radio 2019 96.2 MHz	Dance/R&B	Click on boombox.	www.radio2019.com.tr/
Radio D 104.0 MHz	Turkish Pop		www.dtv.com.tr/radyod.htm
Radyo Bogaziçi 107.9 MHz	Mix/College Radio	Bogaziçi University.	www.radyo.boun.edu.tr/
Radyo Pop 102.8 MHz	Turkish Pop	Click "Live".	www.ntv.com.tr/radyopop/radyopop.htm
Show Radyo 89.9 MHz	Turkish Pop	Click on the red square. Not 24 hours. Inactive?	www.showradyo.com.tr/canli.htm
TGRT-FM 93.1 MHz	Traditional	Click on the CDs.	www.tgrt-fm.com.tr/TgrtSag.htm

Izmir

Radyoaktif 103.5 MHz	Contemp. Hit	Click on the silouette.	www.raksnet.com.tr/radyoaktif/

UKRAINE—Russian

Dnepropetrovsk
Radio Mix 107.3 MHz	Rock		www.rmix.dp.ua/broadcas.htm

UNITED KINGDOM—English

Belfast

Cool FM 97.4 MHz	Variety		www.coolfm.co.uk/news3.htm
BRMB 96.4 MHz	Hits	Select "BRMB OnAir".	www.brmb.co.uk/

Douglas, Isle of Man

Manx Radio 1368 kHz	Variety	Not 24 hours.	www.manxradio.com/audio/live.htm

Ipswich

SGRfm 96.4/97.1 MHz	Pop Rock		www.suffolkweb.co.uk/audio/sir.htm

London

BBC News	World News	Summary. On demand.	news.bbc.co.uk/
BBC Radio 1	Current Shows		www.bbc.co.uk/radio1/listeningbooth/listeningbooth.html
BBC Radio 4	Political News	Occasionally Live.	www.bbc.co.uk/politics97/tvradweb/
BBC Radio 5 909/693 kHz	Current Affairs	Not 24 hours.	www.bbc.co.uk/radio5/live/live.html
BBC World Service	Variety	Live feed, 24-hours.	www.broadcast.com/bbc/
BBC World Service	Variety	~21:05-6:00 Oslo time.	www.nrk.no/alltidnyheter/
BBC World Service	World News	**Multilingual** bulletins.	www.bbc.co.uk/worldservice/
BBC World Service	News & Features	Spanish.	www.clarin.com.ar/
Capital FM 95.8 MHz	Hit Music	Concerts Saturday nights.	www.capitalfm.co.uk/
Capital FM 95.8 MHz	Hit Music	Mirror site.	www.capitalradio.com/
Capital Gold 1548 kHz	Pop		www.capitalgold.co.uk/
Classic FM	Classical	NetShow+RA.	www.classicfm.co.uk/
IBC Tamil Media Ltd.	News & Interviews	**Tamil**. On demand site.	www.ibc-tamil.demon.co.uk/
Independent Radio News	Headlines		www.irn.co.uk/listen.html
interFACE	Alternative	Not 24 hours.	www.pirate-radio.co.uk/interface/live.html
Jazz FM 102.2 MHz	Jazz	Click on "Jazz FM Live". NetShow.	www.jazzfm.co.uk/ms-home.html
Radio Caroline	Rock	On demand site.	www.radiocaroline.co.uk/radio/index.htm
Radio Africa	African	**French**. Music, features.	www.radioafrica.com/radioafrica/programme.html
The Global Channel	Alternative	Not 24 hours.	www.pirate-radio.co.uk/global/live.htm
Virgin Radio 1215 kHz/105.8 MHz	Rock		www.virginradio.co.uk/radio.html
WRN1 English North American Service	International	NetShow.	www.wrn.org/netshow_howto.html
WRN1 English North American Service	International	StreamWorks.	www.wrn.org/streamworks_howto.html
WRN1 English to North America	International		www.wrn.org/realaudio_howto.html
WRN2 Multilingual to North America	International	**Multilingual**.	www.wrn.org/realaudio_howto.html
WRN3 European German Service	International	**German**.	www.wrn.org/realaudio_howto.html

Manchester

Key 103 103.0 MHz	Hits	Click on "Key Live" at lower-left corner.	www.key103fm.com/html/home.html

Norwich
Broadland FM 102.4 MHz — Variety — www.norfolkweb.co.uk/audio/nir.htm

Oldham
Radio LATICS 1566 kHz — Soccer — On demand clips. — members.aol.com/Latics1566/audio.htm

St. Helier, Jersey
Channel 103 FM 103.7 MHz — Rock — www.103fm.itl.net/bcast.html

Wrexham
MFM Music Radio 103.4 MHz — Rock — www.mfmradio.co.uk/

UNITED NATIONS—English

New York
United Nations Radio — News — www.wrn.org/stations/un.html
United Nations Radio — Reports/Briefings — NetShow. — www.internetbroadcast.com/un/

URUGUAY—Spanish

Montevideo
Radio El Espectador 810 kHz — Variety — Click on "Radio en vivo". — www.espectador.com/
Radio Montecarlo CX20 930 kHz — News/Tangos — On demand site. — www.netgate.com.uy/cx20/
Radio Oriental CX12 770 kHz — Soccer — www.netgate.com.uy/cx12/fv.htm
Radio Sarandí CX8 690 kHz — News & Interviews — www.netgate.com.uy/sarandi/

USA—English

Alabama

Athens
WZYP 104.3 MHz — Rock — Click "WZYP Online". — www.wzyp.net/

Auburn
WEGL 91.1 MHz — College Radio — Auburn University. — www.wegl.org/

Birmingham
WEWN (EWTN) — Catholic — Also in **Spanish**. — www.broadcast.com/lightsource/radio/ewtn/index.html
WJOX 690 kHz — Sports — Subject to blackouts. — www.broadcast.com/radio/sports/WJOX/
WRAX 107.7 MHz — Alternative — www.broadcast.com/radio/alternative/WRAX/

Gadsden
WQEN 103.7 MHz — Rock — www.wqen.org/Audio.htm

Huntsville
WOCG 90.1 MHz — Christian — Oakwood College. — www.oakwood.edu/wocg90-1.html
WTKI 1450 kHz — News/Talk/Sports — www.wtki1450.com/

Jacksonville
WLJS "92J" 91.9 MHz — Diverse — Jacksonville State U. — www.jsu.edu/92j/

Mobile
WAVH 106.5 MHz — Oldies — www.wavhfm.com/

Alaska

Fairbanks
KUAC 89.9 MHz — Alaska News — On demand site. — www.uaf.edu/KUAC/FM/sounds.html

Juneau
KINY 800 kHz — News/Variety — www.ptialaska.net/~kiny/kinylive.html

Arizona

Flagstaff
KAFF 92.9 MHz — Country — www.flagstaff.az.us/radio.html
KFLX 105.1 MHz — Quality Rock — www.kflx.com/
KMGN 93.9 MHz — Classic Rock — www.flagstaff.az.us/radio.html

Lake Havesu City
KNLB 91.1 MHz — Religion — www.knlb.com/

Phoenix
BombRadio — Hip-Hop — www.bombradio.com/
CRUX Internet radio — New Rock — crux.marion.org/index.htm

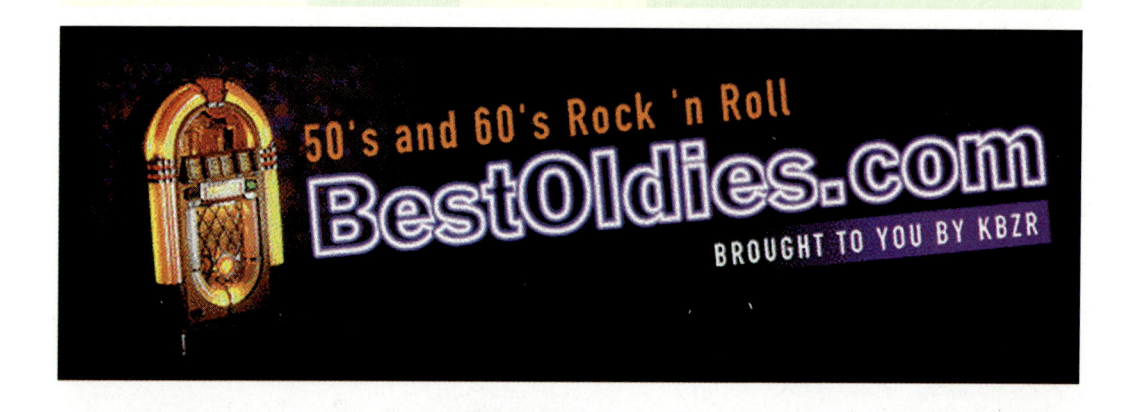

KBZR "The best oldies" 103.9 MHz	Oldies	Arizona-wide network.	www.bestoldies.com/
KMJK "Majik 107" 106.9 MHz	Urban		www.broadcast.com/radio/Urban/KMJK/
KMLE "Camel Country" 107.9	Country		www.broadcast.com/radio/Country/KMLE/

Sedona

KQST 102.9 MHz	Rock	NetShow.	www.kqst.com/default.asp

Arkansas

Conway

KMJX "Magic 105" 105.1MHz	Rock	StreamWorks.	www.magic105fm.com/

Hot Springs

KQUS 97.5 MHz	Country		www.amfm.net/

Little Rock

KKPT 94.1 MHz	Classic Rock		www.kkpt.com/
KSSN "Kissin'" 95.7 MHz	Country	StreamWorks.	www.kssn.com/
KSYG 103.7 MHz	Talk Radio	Not 24 hours.	www.ksyg.com/

Marion

KXHT "Hot 107 FM" 107.1 MHz	Hip-Hop/R&B		www.broadcast.com/radio/urban/KXHT/

Russellville

KXRJ 91.9 MHz	College Radio	Arkansas Technical U.	broadcast.atu.edu/

California

Arcata

KRFH Radio Free Humboldt	College Radio	Humboldt State U.	www.humboldt.edu/~krfh/realaudio.html

Berkeley

Radio Free Berkeley 104.1 MHz	Alternative	Low power micro station. Experimental operation.	radio.transbay.net:7070/ramgen/bleah.ra

Brawley

KSIQ "Q96" 96.1 MHz	Rock		www.digitalwave.net/q96/

Brisbane

Imagine Radio	Wide Variety	Requires installation of "Imagine Radio"	www.imagineradio.com/pods/welcome/

Cambria

KOTR "The Otter" 94.9 MHz	Rhythm 'n Blues	Select "Spinning Now".	www.kotrfm.com/
KOTR "The Otter" 94.9 MHz	Rhythm 'n Blues	StreamWorks at this URL:	www.radiodayz.com/kotter/

Carmel

New Radio Star	Soft Rock	StreamWorks+RA.	www.newradiostar.com/

Chico

KZAP "The Rock" 96.7 MHz	Classic Rock		www.kzap.com/

Cupertino

All India Internet Radio	Features	On demand. Also **Hindi**.	www.aiir.com/
KKUP "People's Radio" 91.5 MHz	Diverse	On demand site.	www.kkup.com/audio.html

Dana Point

American Pacific Techno Network	News & Music	**Vietnamese**. Many links.	ampact.net/apradio/

Davis

KDVS 90.3 MHz	College Radio	U. of California, Davis.	www.kdvs.org/
KQBR "The Breeze" 104.3 MHz	Urban		www.broadcast.com/radio/Urban/KQBR/

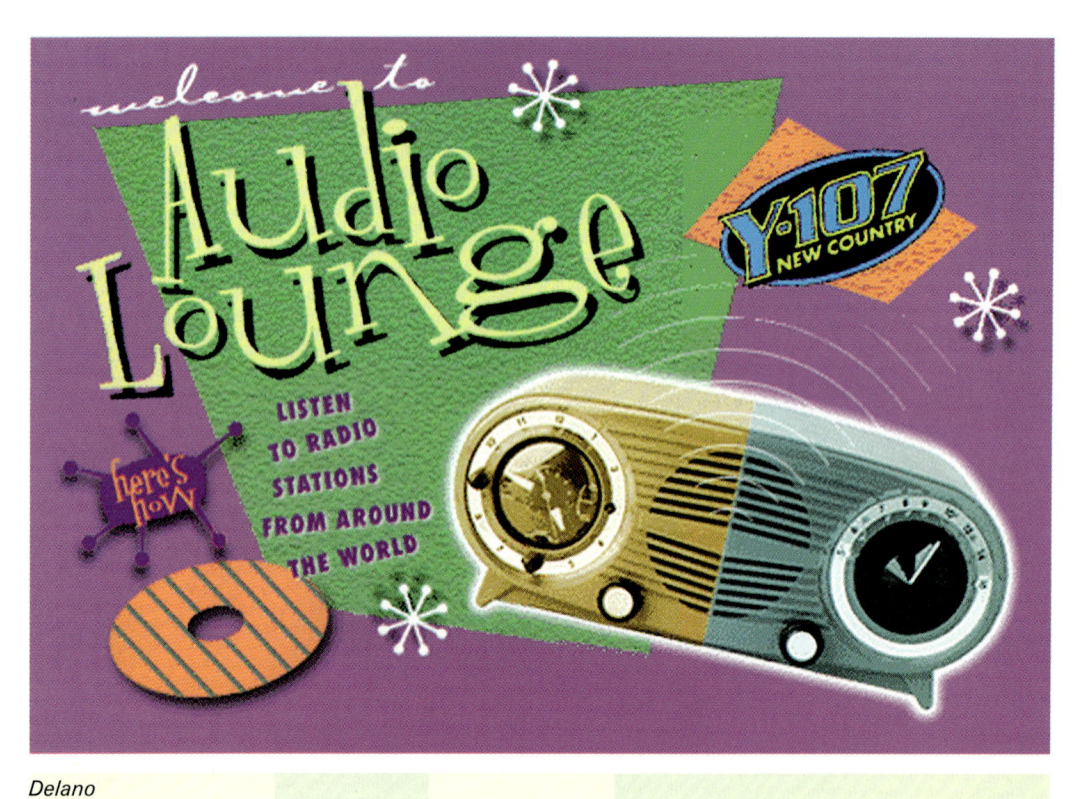

Welcome to Audio Lounge
Listen to radio stations from around the world

Delano
KDNO 98.5 MHz	Religion		www.truthradio.com/
KMAK "Truth Radio" 100.3 MHz	Christian Talk		www.truthradio.com/

El Cajon
KHTS "Channel 933" 93.3 MHz	Dance		www.channel933.com/

Freedom
KPIG 107.5 MHz	Original Blend	StreamWorks+RA.	www.kpig.com/live1.htm

Fremont
KUFX "K-FOX" 104.9 MHz	Classic Rock	NetShow.	www.kufx.com/

Fresno
KBOS "B95" 94.9 MHz	Top 40		www.broadcast.com/radio/top_40/KBOS/
KCBL "The Ball" 1340 kHz	Sports	Subject to blackouts.	www.broadcast.com/radio/Sports/KCBL/
KFRR "New Rock" 104.1 MHz	Alternative		www.broadcast.com/radio/Alternative/KFRR/
KJFX "The Fox" 95.7 MHz	Classic Rock		www.broadcast.com/radio/classic_rock/KJFX/
KMJ 580 kHz	News Talk		www.broadcast.com/radio/Talk/KMJ/
KNAX "Kickin' Country" 97.9 MHz	Country		www.broadcast.com/radio/Country/KNAX/
KRZR 103.7 MHz	Rock		www.broadcast.com/radio/Rock/KRZR/
KSKS "Kiss" 93.7 MHz	Country		www.broadcast.com/radio/Country/KSKS/
KVSR "Star 101" 101.1 MHz	Album		www.broadcast.com/radio/adult_album_alternative/KVSR/
KYNO "Big 13" 1300 kHz	Sports		www.broadcast.com/radio/Sports/KYNO/

Garberville
KHUM 104.7/104.3 MHz	Original Mix		www.khum.com/live.htm
KMUD 91.1 MHz	Diverse	Redwood Community R.	www.kmud.org/audio.html

Garden Grove
VietNam California Radio (VNCR)	News & Info	Vietnamese.	kicon.com/VNCR/
VOV (Voice of Vietnamese) Radio	News	Vietnamese.	www.vovradio.com/

Gilroy
KBAY "The Bay" 94.5 MHz	Soft Rock	NetShow.	www.kbay.com/

Glendale
Christian Pirate Radio	Christian	Affiliated with KKLA. NetShow+RA.	www.broadcast.com/lightsource/radio/pirate/canvas.html

Grover Beach
RadioDayz	Future Rock	StreamWorks.	www.radiodayz.com/radiostation/dayzradio/index.htm

Hanford
KIGS 620 kHz	News/Pop	Portuguese.	www.kigs.com/return.htm

Hayward
KSUH 880 kHz	College Radio	California State Univ.	www.broadcast.com/radio/College/KSUH/

Hollister
KCDU "CD93" 93.5 MHz	Adult Contemp.	Click on "webcast".	www.cd93.com/

Irwindale
Asian American Network	Variety	Chinese. For live audio, click far right button.	www.radiochina.com/index_ra_js.htm

Lancaster
KAVL 610 kHz	Sports		www.broadcast.com/radio/Sports/KAVL/
KHJJ 1380 kHz	Talk Radio	Subject to blackouts.	www.broadcast.com/radio/Talk/KHJJ/

Los Altos
KFJC 89.7 MHz	College Radio	Requires download of GTS Audio software.	www.kfjc.org/

Los Angeles
KBLA 1580 kHz "Radio Korea"	News & Info	Korean.	www.radiokorea.com/
KFI 640 kHz	News Talk		www.kfi640.com/programming/index.html
KIIS 102.7 MHz	Rock		www.kiisfm.com/
KKLA 1240 kHz/99.5 MHz	Christian		www.broadcast.com/lightsource/radio/kkla/
KLVE 107.5 MHz	Latino	Spanish. Click KLVE.	www.h-span.net/usa.htm
KXTA 1150 kHz	Sports	Poor audio quality.	www.am1150.com/live.htm
KXTA "SportsRadio LA" 1150	Sports		www.am1150.com/live.htm
KZLA 93.9 MHz	Country		www.kzla.net/listen.htm
LiveConcerts Cybercast	Rock Concerts	Live events and archive.	www.liveconcerts.com/

Rock performances are available live and on-demand from Los Angeles via LiveConcerts.

Mojave			
KAVS 97.7 MHz	Rock		www.rock977.com/
Moreno Valley			
KHPY 1530 kHz	Oldies	Occasional live program.	www.annetta.com/khpy/
Oakland			
Family Radio	Christian	Via KEAR San Francisco.	www.familyradio.com/
Pismo Beach			
KWBR 95.3 MHz	Rock	StreamWorks.	www.kwbrfm.com/startlisten.htm
Pomona			
KMNY 1600 kHz	Business	Chinese 4PM-4AM.	www.money-radio.com/monrad/MRmain.htm
San Clemente			
KWVE 107.9	Religion		www.kwve.org/broadcast/index.htm
San Diego			
CTSNET ON-AIR	Pop/Rock/Dance	*Three* programs.	www.on-air.com/
KBZT "K-Best 95" 94.9 MHz	Oldies	Click RealAudio logo.	www.kbest.com/
KCR San Diego State University	College Radio	San Diego State U.	kahuna.sdsu.edu/kcr/
KFMB-AM 760 kHz	Talk Radio		www.760kfmb.com/
KFMB-FM "Star" 100.7 MHz	Classic 80s/90s		www.histar.com/
KGB 101.5 MHz	Album Rock		www.101kgb.com/topradio1.html
KIFM "Jazz FM" 98.1 MHz	Smooth Jazz		www.kifm.com/
KOGO 600 kHz	Talk Radio		www.broadcast.com/radio/Talk/KOGO/
KPLN "The Planet" 103.7 MHz	Classic Rock	NetShow.	www.broadcast.com/radio/classic_rock/kpln/
KSDO 1130 kHz	Talk Radio	Subject to blackouts.	www.broadcast.com/radio/Talk/KSDO/
KSDS "Jazz 88" 88.3 MHz	Jazz	Click RealAudio logo.	209.133.12.76/Jazz88/index.html
KSON 97.3 MHz	Country		www.kson.com/lisnlive.htm
KYXY 96.5 MHz	Adult Contemp.	NetShow.	www.broadcast.com/radio/adult_contemporary/kyxy/
XETRA-AM 690 kHz	Sports	Transmits from Tijuana.	www.broadcast.com/radio/sports/xtra/index.html
XETRA-FM "91X" 91.1 MHz	Rock	Transmits from Tijuana.	www.91x.com/
XHRM "The Flash" 92.5 MHz	Alternative Rock	Transmits from Tijuana.	www.92five.com/
XHITZ "Z90" 90.3 MHz	Top 40/Hip-Hop	Transmits from Tijuana.	www.z90.com/
San Dimas			
Internet Ki Awaz	Pakistani Music	Aadab **Urdu** Community.	www.ipgeek.com/Default.html
San Francisco			
KEAR 106.9 MHz	Christian	Family Radio network.	www.thegospel.com/cntidx.htm
KKSF 103.7 MHz	Smooth Jazz	NetShow.	www.audiolounge.com/stream/providers/kksf/
KNBR 680 kHz	Sports		www.broadcast.com/radio/Sports/KNBR/
KUSF 90.3 MHz	Eclectic/Ethnic	U. of San Francisco.	www.usfca.edu/kusf/
San Jose			
Da Coconut Wireless	Hawaiian		www.punawelewele.com/cocontyrls/
KSJO 92.3 MHz	Solid Rock	NetShow.	www.ksjo.com/
KVCH 104.1 MHz	Christian College		kvch.valleychristian.net/
Lao Waves	Songs and Music	Laotian. On demand.	www.laowaves.com/
VNFM (VIETNAM FM 96.1)	Music/News/Talk	Vietnamese.	www.vnmedia.com/webcast/
San Luis Obispo			
KLFF "K-Life" 89.3 MHz	Contem. Christian	StreamWorks.	www.klife.org/
San Mateo			
KCSM 91.1 MHz	Jazz		www.kcsm.org/jazz91.html
KTCT "The Ticket" 1050 kHz	Sports		www.broadcast.com/radio/Sports/KTCT/

Santa Ana
Little Saigon Radio	News Talk	Vietnamese.	littlesaigonradio.com/
Music Radio	Traditional/Pop	Vietnamese.	kicon.com/musicradio/
Trinity Broadcasting	Religion		www.tbn.org/media.htm

Santa Monica
KCRW 89.9 MHz	Eclectic/NPR	Subject to blackouts.	kcrw.org/live/
KCRW 89.9 MHz	Rock Concerts	On demand site.	www.liveconcerts.com/listening/kcrw/
KRSI (Radio Sedaye Iran)	News/Features	Farsi. NetShow.	www.krsi.com/default.asp

Santa Rosa
KLVR "K-LOVE" 91.9 MHz	Christian	NetShow+RA.	klove.com/Webpages/live.html

Stanford
KZSU 90.1 MHz	College Radio	Stanford University.	realaudio.stanford.edu/

Stockton
KCJH 90.1 MHz	Christian		www.kcjh.com/link.htm

Sunland
Cable Radio Network (CRN)	Adult Contemp.		www.broadcast.com/radio/contemporary/crn/

Twain Harte
KKBN 93.5 MHz	Soft Hits		www.cabinradio.com/realaudio.htm

Twentynine Palms
KCDZ 107.7 MHz	Adult Contemp.		www.virtual29.com/z107/links.html

Valencia
KCIA 105.3 MHz	Freeform	California Institute of Arts.	shoko.calarts.edu/~kcia/

Ventura
KLYY "Y-107" 107.1 MHz	Modern Rock	NetShow.	www.audioactive.com/listen/providers/klyy/

Westminster
Saigon Radio	News & Info	Vietnamese.	www.saigonradio.com/

Woodland Hills
Vortex Technology "Vortex Live"	Talk/Entertainment	StreamWorks.	www.vortex.com/av1.html

Yucaipa
KLRD 90.1 MHz (Air-1 Radio)	Christian		www.air1radio.com/

Colorado

Boulder
GoGaGa Brand Radio	Freeform Eclectic	Eclectic Radio Co.	www.gogaga.com/
KGNU 88.5 MHz	Alternative	Community Radio.	www.kgnu.org/
Radio M	Mixed Bag	Eclectic Radio Co.	www.radiom.com/

Boulder City
KQOL 105.5 MHz "KOOL Radio"	Oldies		www.vegasradio.com/kool.html

Colorado Springs
KEPC 89.7 MHz	College Radio	Pikes Peak Community College	www.ppcc.cccoes.edu/dept/kepc/
KILO 94.3 MHz	Alternative		www.broadcast.com/radio/Alternative/KILO

Grand Junction
KSTR "K-Star" 96.1 MHz	Classic Rock		www.kstr.com/sample.htm

Johnstown
KHNC 1360 kHz	Talk Radio	American Freedom Net. StreamWorks.	www.amerifree.com/

Oak Creek
KFMU 104.1 MHz | Rock | Select "SPINNING NOW". | www.kfmu.com/

Widefield
KKLI 106.3 MHz | Lite Rock | | kkli.com/virtual.htm

Connecticut

Bolton
Reno's WEB Site | Freeform | Live Saturday nights. | www.tiac.net/users/renoct/scripts/live.htm

Bristol
ESPN Sports Zone | Sports Features | | espn.sportszone.com/editors/liveaudio/index.html

Greenwich
WGCH 1490 kHz | Variety | Click on the globe. StreamWorks. | www.internetwork.com/radio1.htm

Hamden
WKCI 101.3 MHz | Hits | | www.kc101.com/

Hartford
KJSS 95.7 MHz | Rock | | www.kiss957.com/KISSRA/kissra.html
WDRC 102.9 kHz | Oldies | | www.wdrc.com/fm.html
WDRC 1360 kHz | Pop & News | | www.wdrc.com/am.html
WHCN 105.9 | Classic Rock | | www.1059hcn.com/
WKSS 95.7 MHz | Hits | | www.kiss957.com/KISSRA/kissra.html
WPOP 1410 kHz | Sports | NetShow. | www.broadcast.com/radio/sports/WPOP/

New Haven
WPLR "99 Rock" 99.1 MHz | Rock | NetShow. | www.broadcast.com/radio/Rock/WPLR/
WYBC 94.3 MHz | Urban | NetShow. | www.broadcast.com/radio/Urban/WYBC/

Norwalk
WEFX "The Fox" 95.9 MHz | Classic Hits | StreamWorks. | www.internetwork.com/radio2.htm

Stamford
WKHL 96.7 MHz | Oldies | StreamWorks. | www.internetwork.com/radio3.htm

Waterbury
WMRQ 104.1 MHz | Rock | NetShow. | www.broadcast.com/radio/rock/WMRQ/
WWYZ 92.5 MHz | Country | NetShow. | www.broadcast.com/radio/country/WWYZ/

West Hartford
WWUH 91.3 MHz	College Radio	University of Hartford.	www.hartford.edu/wwuh/ra.html

Delaware
Georgetown
WZBH "The Beach" 93.5 MHz	Rock	Click arrow at lower-right.	www.ce.net/wzbh/

Wilmington
WDEL 1150 kHz	News Talk		www.wdel.com/listen.htm
WJBR 99.5 MHz	MOR Pop		www.wjbr.com/wjbr.htm

District of Columbia
Washington
ANA Radio (Arab-Net)	Arab-American	Arabic.	www.anaradio.com/
C-SPAN & C-SPAN 2	Public Affairs	*Two* live programs.	www.broadcast.com/radio/tv/c-span/
C-SPAN via WCSP 90.1 MHz	Public Affairs		www.c-span.org/radio90x.htm
National Public Radio (NPR)	Features	On demand site.	www.realaudio.com/contentp/npr.html
National Public Radio (NPR)	News/Reports	On demand site.	www.npr.org/news/
Radio Free Asia	News & Info	Multilingual.	www.rfa.org
Radio Free Europe/Radio Liberty	News & Info	Multilingual.	www.rferl.org/realaudio/index.html
Voice of America	News & Features	Click "Listen to VOA Live!"	www.voa-afl.org/
Voice of America	News & Features	Multilingual.	www.voa.gov/programs/audio/realaudio/
VOA "Communications World"	News & Info	On demand site.	www.wrn.org/voa.html
VOA "News Now"	News	Direct URL:	www.voa.gov/audio.ram
WETA 90.9 MHz	Features	On demand site.	www.weta.org/fm/audio.html
WMET 1150 kHz	Business		www.broadcast.com/radio/business/wmet/index.html
WPFW 89.3 MHz	Jazz/Ethnic		www.capcity.com/wpfwradio/

Florida
Boca Raton
WOWL 91.7 MHz	College Radio	Florida Atlantic Univ.	www.fau.edu/wowl/

Fort Lauderdale
WFTL 1400 kHz	Talk Radio		www.broadcast.com/radio/Talk/WFTL/

Jacksonville
Music Choice	Ten Programs	StreamWorks. Cable modem or ISDN required.	www.jacksonville.net/closetohome/town/music/music_choice/mchoice/index.html
WAPE 95.1 MHz	Top 40	NetShow.	www.broadcast.com/radio/top_40/WAPE/
WBWL "The Ball" 600 kHz	Sports	NetShow.	www.broadcast.com/radio/sports/wbwl/
WFYV "Rock 105" 104.5 MHz	Classic Rock	NetShow.	www.broadcast.com/radio/classic_rock/wfyv/
WKOV 690 kHz	Talk Radio	NetShow.	www.broadcast.com/radio/talk/wokv/
WKQL "Cool" 96.9 MHz	Oldies	NetShow.	www.broadcast.com/radio/oldies/wkql/
WMXQ "Mix 103" 102.9 MHz	Adult Contemp.	NetShow.	www.broadcast.com/radio/adult_contemporary/wmxq/
WNZS 930 kHz	Sports	Subject to blackouts.	www.broadcast.com/radio/Sports/WNZS/
WPLA "Planet Radio" 93.3 MHz	Alternative		www.broadcast.com/radio/alternative/WPLA/
WROO "Rooster" 107.3 MHz	Country		www.broadcast.com/radio/Country/WROO/
WZNZ 1460 kHz	News		www.broadcast.com/radio/News/WZNZ/

Lakeland
WSJT "Smooth Jazz" 94.1 MHz	Smooth Jazz		www.broadcast.com/radio/Jazz/WSJT/

Web radio is the ultimate for keeping up with local news in cities worldwide. WHNZ covers news, weather and sports for the entire Tampa Bay area.

570 AM WHNZ
News & Talk for Tampa Bay

Largo
WZTM "The Team" 820 kHz	Sports	Subject to blackouts.	www.broadcast.com/radio/Sports/WZTM/

Macclenny
WJXR "Bargain Channel" 92.1	Shopping		www.wjxr.com/

Miami
Miami Christian University	Religion		cirnet.com/stations/mcu.htm
Templo de Rey Jesús	Christian	Spanish.	cirnet.com/stations/tdrj.htm
WAMR "Amor" 107.5 MHz	Love Songs	Spanish.	www.wamr.com/Audio.html
WAQI "Radio Mambi" 710 kHz	Cuban/Latin Music	Spanish.	www.waqi.com/Audio.html
WINZ 940 kHz	News		www.broadcast.com/radio/News/WINZ/
WIOD 610 kHz	News/Talk/Sports	Subject to blackouts.	www.broadcast.com/radio/Talk/WIOD/
WLVE "Love 94" 93.9 MHz	Smooth Jazz		www.broadcast.com/radio/Jazz/WLVE/
WMCU 89.7 MHz	Christian	Trinity International U.	www.wmcuradio.com/
WPLL "Planet Radio" 103.5 MHz	Alternative		www.broadcast.com/radio/alternative/WPLL/
WQAM 560 kHz	Sports		www.broadcast.com/radio/Sports/WQAM/
WQBA 1140 kHz	Cuban	Spanish.	www.wqba.com/Audio.html
WRTO 98.3 MHz	Salsa/Merengue	Spanish.	www.wrto.com/
WSUA 1260 kHz Caracol-Miami	Latino	Spanish.	www.caracolusa.com/
WTMI 93.1 MHz	Classical		www.wtmi.com/realaudio.html
WZTA "ZETA" 94.9 MHz	Rock		www.broadcast.com/radio/Rock/WZTA/

Miami Beach
WMBM 1490 kHz	Gospel		cirnet.com/stations/wmbm.htm

Orlando
WDBO 580 kHz	Talk Radio	Subject to blackouts.	www.broadcast.com/radio/Talk/WDBO/
WJRR 101.1 MHz	Rock		www.broadcast.com/radio/Rock/WJRR/
WMGF "Magic" 107.7 MHz	Soft Easy Favorites		www.broadcast.com/radio/Adult_Contemporary/WMGF/
WPRD "La Fantástica" 1440 kHz	Salsa/Merengue	Spanish.	www.broadcast.com/radio/International/WPRD/
WRLZ "Radio Luz" 1270 kHz	Christian	Spanish.	wrlzradioluz.com/
WSHE 100.3 MHz	Adult Contemp.		www.broadcast.com/radio/adult_contemporary/WSHE/
WTKS "REAL Radio" 104.1 MHz	Talk Radio		www.broadcast.com/radio/Talk/WTKS/
WWNZ 740 kHz	News		www.broadcast.com/radio/News/WWNZ/

Panama City
WFSY "Sunny" 98.5 MHz	Adult Contemp.		www.broadcast.com/radio/adult_contemporary/WFSY/
WPAP 92.5 MHz	Country		www.broadcast.com/radio/Country/WPAP/
WSHF 99.3 MHz	Alternative		www.broadcast.com/radio/alternative/WSHF/

Pensacola
WTKX "TK 101" 101.5 MHz	Rock		www.broadcast.com/radio/Rock/WTKX/
WYCL "Cool-107" 107.3 MHz	Oldies		www.broadcast.com/radio/Oldies/WYCL/

Pine Hills
| WQTM "The Team" 540 kHz | Sports | Subject to blackouts. | www.broadcast.com/radio/Sports/WQTM/ |

Port St. Lucie
| WPSL 1590 kHz | Talk Radio | | www.broadcast.com/radio/Talk/WPSL/ |

St. Augustine
| WFSJ "Smooth Jazz" 97.9 MHz | Smooth Jazz | | www.broadcast.com/radio/Jazz/WFSJ/ |

St. Petersburg
| WCOF "Coast 107.3" | Classic Rock | | www.broadcast.com/radio/classic_rock/wcof/ |

South Beach
| WOMB 107.1 MHz | Electronic Radio | Micro broadcaster. | thewomb.com/main.htm |

Tallahassee
WJZT "Smooth Jazz" 100.7 MHz	Smooth Jazz		www.broadcast.com/radio/Jazz/WJZT/
WNLS 1270 kHz	Sports	Subject to blackouts.	www.broadcast.com/radio/Sports/WNLS/
WSNI "Sunny 107" 107.1 MHz	Oldies		www.broadcast.com/radio/Oldies/WSNI/
WTNT 94.9 MHz	Country		www.broadcast.com/radio/Country/WTNT/
WXSR 101.5 MHz	Alternative		www.broadcast.com/radio/alternative/WXSR/

Tampa
Pirate Radio Network 102.1 FM	Rock 'n' Roll		www.ldbrewer.com/pirate.html
WDAE 1250 kHz	Sports		www.broadcast.com/radio/sports/wdae/
WFLA 970 kHz	News Talk	Subject to blackouts.	www.broadcast.com/radio/News/WFLA/
WHNZ 570 kHz	News	Subject to blackouts.	www.broadcast.com/radio/News/WHNZ/
WHPT "The Point" 102.5 MHz	Album		www.broadcast.com/radio/adult_album_alternative/whpt/
WMNF 88.5 MHz	Community Radio		audio.wmnf.org/
WMTX "Star" 95.7 MHz	Adult Contemp.		www.broadcast.com/radio/adult_contemporary/WMTX/

Tampa Bay
| WILV "Love" 101.5 MHz | Adult Contemp. | | www.broadcast.com/radio/contemporary/WILV/ |

White Springs
| United Broadcasting Network (UBN) | Talk Radio | | www.broadcast.com/radio/talk/ubn/ |

Georgia

Atlanta
CNN Audioselect	News	*Five* networks, including sports, and **Spanish**.	www.cnn.com/audioselect/
WGST 640 kHz/105.7 MHz	News		www.broadcast.com/radio/News/WGST/
WJZF "Jazz Flavors" 104.1 MHz	Smooth Jazz	Not 24 hours.	www.accessatlanta.com/wjzf/index.html
WKLS "96 Rock" 96.1 MHz	Rock		www.broadcast.com/radio/Rock/WKLS/
WNNX "99X" 99.7 MHz	Alternative		www.com/99x/program.html

For national and international news, Atlanta's CNN is great. But to know what's going on *in* Atlanta, turn to WGST-AM. Both are on Web radio.

WQXI "The Zone" 790 kHz	Sports		www.broadcast.com/radio/sports/wqxi/
WREK 91.1 MHz	Diverse	Georgia Tech.	www.gatech.edu/wrek/
WSB 750 kHz	Talk Radio	Subject to blackouts.	www.broadcast.com/radio/Talk/WSB/
WSTR "Star 94" 94.1 MHz	Hits	NetShow.	www.star94.com/sounds/sounds.html

Cartersville
Immanuel Broadcasting Network	Christian		www.ibnetwork.org/live.html

Columbus
WRCG 1420 kHz	News Talk		www.preferred-computers.com/Radio_Show/radio_show.html

Gainesville
WMJE "Magic" 102.9 MHz	Hits	Click "Hear Us Live".	www.wmje.com/

Savannah
WAEV 97.3 MHz	Rock		www.mix973.com/

Hawai'i

Honolulu, Oahu
KIKI 93.9 MHz	Rock		www.i-94.net/live.html

Kailua, Oahu
Internet Radio Hawaii	Hawaiian	On demand site.	hotspots.hawaii.com/irhmusic2.html

Kihei, Maui
KONI 104.7 MHz	Hits		www.mauigateway.com/~koni/live.htm

Lahaina, Maui
KPOA 93.5 MHz	Contem. Hawaiian		www.mauigateway.com/~kpoa/page6.html

Lihue, Kauai
KQNG "Kong" 93.5 MHz/ 570 kHz	Hawaiian Variety		www.kongradio.com/live.html

Idaho

Boise
KBSU 90.3 MHz	Jazz	Boise State University.	www.idbsu.edu/bsuradio/bsuaudio.htm

Caldwell
KTSY 89.5 MHz	Contem. Christian		www.ktsy.org/intro.htm

Illinois

Carbondale
WIDB 104.3 MHz	College Radio	SIU - Carbondale.	www.siu.edu/~widb/

Champaign
WBGL 91.7 MHz	Contem. Christian		www.wbgl.org/realaudio.html
WEBX-FM 93.5 MHz	Adult Album Altern.		www.webxfm.com/webaudio.html

Chicago
Flames Radio 89.5 MHz	Freeform	U. of Illinois - Chicago.	www.flamesradio.com/hear.htm

Rebel Radio	Hard Rock	6:00 PM-6:00 AM CST.	www.rebelradio.com/reblram.html
Sunlite Radio	Christian	On demand music site.	www.sunlite-radio.com/
WCBR "Cyber Radio 927"	Dance	On demand site.	www.cyberradio927.com/about.html
WFMT 98.7 MHz	Classical		www.broadcast.com/radio/Classical/WFMT/
WGN 720 kHz	Talk Radio		www.wgnradio.com/
WHCI "Hellenic Radio"	Ethnic	Greek. Transmitted as SCA over WGCI-FM.	www.hellenicradio.com/live.html
WLS 890 kHz	Talk Radio	NetShow.	www.wlsam.com/wls/message.html
WMBI 1110 kHz/90.1 MHz	Christian	StreamWorks.	www.broadcast.com/lightsource/radio/wmbi/
WMBI 1110 kHz/90.1 MHz	Christian	StreamWorks+RA.	www.mbn.org/MBN/WMBI/
WMVP 1000 kHz	Sports	Chicago Bulls. NetShow.	www.am1000.com/tuner.html
WMVP 1000 kHz	Talk Radio		www.broadcast.com/radio/Talk/WMVP/
WXCD 94.7 MHz	Classic Rock	NetShow.	www.audioactive.com/listen/providers/wxcd/

Jerseyville
WALC "Alice@104.1" 104.1 MHz	Adult Alternative		aliceinstlouis.com/

Kankakee
WONU 89.7 MHz	Contem. Christian	Olivet Nazarene Univ.	www.wonu.org/

Morris
WCFL 104.7 MHz	Contem. Christian		www.wcfl.com/

Normal
WIHN 96.7 MHz	Rock		www.i-97.com/live.htm

Peoria
WSWT 106.9 MHz	Lite Rock		www.literock107.com/
WWCT 105.7 MHz "Rock 106"	Rock	NetShow+RA.	www.rock106.com/listen.htm
WXCL 104.9 MHz	Country		www.wxcl.com/WXCLListenLive.htm

Taylorville
WMKR 94.3 MHz	Lite Rock	Click on the rooster.	www.chipsnet.com/index.html-ssi

Vernon Hills
WNVR 1030 kHz	International	Multilingual.	www.pclradio.com/index.html

Wheaton
WETN 88.1 MHz	Christian	Wheaton College.	www.wheaton.edu/wetn/Audio.htm

Indiana

Evansville
WIKY "104FM" 104.1 MHz	Hits	NetShow.	www.wiky.com/newsite2/index2.html
WUEV 91.5 MHz	College Radio	Univ. of Evansville. StreamWorks.	cedar.evansville.edu/~wuevweb/netcast/

Fort Wayne
WBCL 90.3 MHz	Christian Music	Taylor U. NetShow +RA.	www.wbcl.org/
WLAB 88.3 MHz	Religion/Rock		www.wlab.org/

WIBC-AM 1070 is the best source of news about Indiana on the Web.

Indianapolis

WFBQ "Q95" 94.7 MHz	Rock	NetShow.	www.audioactive.com/listen/providers/wfbq/
WGRL "The Bear" 93.9 MHz	New Hit Country		www.wgrl.com/
WIBC 1070 kHz	Talk Radio		www.wibc.com/wibcfeed.html
WNDE 1260 kHz	Sports	NetShow.	www.broadcast.com/radio/sports/wnde/
WRZX 103.3 MHz	Alternative	NetShow.	http://www.broadcast.com/radio/alternative/wrzx/
WTLC "Gold Soul" 1310 kHz	Urban	Off-air relay.	www.broadcast.com/radio/Urban/WTLCam/
WTLC "Power" 105.7 MHz	Urban		www.broadcast.com/radio/urban/wtlc/

Roanoke

WYSR "Star" 94.1 MHz	Modern Hits		www.star941.com/

Scottsburg

WMPI 105.3 MHz	Country		www.scottsburg.com/main.htm

South Bend

World Harvest Radio International (LeSEA Broadcasting); carried over shortwave stations WHRI (South Bend), KWHR (Naalehu, Hawai'i), and WHRA (Greenbush, Maine).	Christian	*Five* audio feeds. Also Spanish and Asian Multilingual content. Carries paid programming, including Radio Free Asia.	www.whr.org/realaudio.htm
WHME "Harvest" 103.1 MHz	Christian/Sports	Notre Dame football.	www.lesea.com/lesea2/realaudio.htm
WHPZ/WGTC 96.9/102.3 MHz	Christian Rock	Select "Pulse FM".	www.lesea.com/lesea2/realaudio.htm

Iowa

Belle Plaine

KZAT 95.5 MHz	Yesterday's Hits		www.kzat.com/

Centerville

KMGO "99 Country" 98.7 MHz	Country		www.broadcast.com/radio/Country/KMGO/

Mason City

KLSS "Mix 106" 106.1 MHz	Rock		www.klssradio.com/

Kansas

Hays

KJLS "Mix 103" 103.3 MHz	Rock		www.mix103fm.com/

Kansas City

KCHZ 95.7 MHz	New Music		www.channelz95.com/z95/asp/real.asp
WDAF 610 kHz	Country		www.tfs.net/wdafaudio/audio.html
KQRC "The Rock" 98.9 MHz	Rock		989therock.com/main.html

Lawrence

KJHK "The Hawk" 90.7 MHz	College Radio	University of Kansas.	www.broadcast.com/radio/College/KJHK/

Leavenworth
KKLO 1410 kHz	**Religion**		www.kklo.com/audio.html

Manhattan
KKSU 580 kHz	**College Radio**	Kansas State Univ. Weekday evenings.	www.oznet.ksu.edu/kksu/

Topeka
WIBW 580 kHz	**Country**	Mornings and weekends.	www.oznet.ksu.edu/kksu/

Wichita
KFDI-AM 1070 kHz	**Country**		www.broadcast.com/radio/country/kfdiam/
KFDI-FM 101.3 MHz	**Country**		www.broadcast.com/radio/country/kfdifm/
KICT "T-95" 95.1 MHz	**Rock**		www.broadcast.com/radio/rock/kict/
KKRD 107.3 MHz	**Hits**	NetShow.	www.1073kkrd.com/
KLLS 104.5 MHz	**Hits Of The 70's**		www.broadcast.com/radio/contemporary_hits/klls/
KNSS 1240 kHz	**News Talk/Sports**	NetShow.	www.broadcast.com/radio/talk/KNSS/
KRZZ 96.3 MHz	**Rock**	NetShow.	www.krzz.com/menu.html
KTLI 99.1 MHz	**Comtem. Christian**		www.southwind.net/ktli/live.html
KYQQ 106.5 MHz	**Hot Country**		www.broadcast.com/radio/country/kyqq/
KZZD "Z91" 90.7 MHz	**Christian Rock**		www.z91.org/RealAudio.htm

Kentucky

Lexington
WVLK 590 kHz	News/Talk/Sports		www.wvlkam.com/schedule.html

Shelbyville
WTHQ "Thunder" 101.7 MHz	Country		www.sky1.net/thunder/

Louisiana

Coushatta
KSBH "The River" 94.9 MHz	Country		www.ksbh.com/

Hammond
KSLU 90.9 MHz	College Radio	Southeastern Louisiana U.	www.broadcast.com/radio/College/KSLU/

Houma
KCIL "C107 FM" 107.5 MHz	Country		www.c107.com/realaudio.html

New Orleans
Radio Free New Orleans	Jazz/Funky	New Orleans Tourism.	www.neworleansonline.com/rfno.htm
WBSN 89.1 MHz	Christian	NetShow.	www.lifesongs.com/live.html
WWOZ 90.7 MHz	Jazz	Music of New Orleans.	www.broadcast.com/radio/Jazz/WWOZ/

Shreveport
KEEL 710 kHz	News/Talk/Sports		www.broadcast.com/radio/talk/keel/
KITT 93.7 MHz	Country		www.broadcast.com/radio/country/kitt/
KWKH 1130 kHz	News/Talk/Sports		www.broadcast.com/radio/sports/kwkh/
WRUF 94.5 MHz	Top 40		www.broadcast.com/radio/top_40/kruf/

Maine

Lewiston
WRBC 91.5 MHz	College Radio	Bates College.	www.bates.edu/wrbc/listen.html

Maryland

Annapolis
WRNR 103.1 MHz	Freeform		www.wrnr.com/

Baltimore
Navrang Radio	News/Music	S. Asian **Multilingual**.	www.broadcast.com/radio/international/navrangradio/
WBAL "Radio 11" 1090 kHz	Talk Radio		www.broadcast.com/radio/Talk/WBAL/
WCBM 680 kHz	News		wcbm.com/content.html
WEAA 88.9 MHz	Multicultural	Morgan State Univ.	www.morgan.edu/geninfo/weaa.htm
WIYY "98 Rock" 97.9 MHz	Rock		www.broadcast.com/radio/Rock/WIYY/
WRBS 95.1 MHz	Christian		www.wrbs.com/

Bethesda
WTEM "The Team" 570 kHz	Sports		www.broadcast.com/radio/Sports/WTEM/

College Park
WMUC 650 kHz	Rock/Top 40	Univ. of Maryland.	www.wmuc.umd.edu/real/
WMUC 88.1 MHz	Freeform	Univ. of Maryland.	www.wmuc.umd.edu/real/

Grasonville
WRNR 103.1 MHz	Progressive		www.wrnr.com/

Laurel
Maranatha Internet Radio	Contem. Christian	Click "Live Music…"	www.maranatha.net/jukebox/

Potomac
WCTN 950 kHz	Religion		www.wctn.net/

Silver Spring
Adventist World Radio | **Religion/Info** | Multilingual. | www.awr.org/audio/online_programs.html
Muslim Television Ahmadiyya | **Islamic** | English/Urdu. | alislam.org/audio/

Takoma Park
WGTS 91.9 MHz | **Christian** | | www.cuc.edu/~wgts/real.html

Massachusetts
Amherst
WFCR 88.5 MHz | **Classical/Jazz** | Not live 24 hours. | www.wfcr.org/

Boston
WEEI 850 kHz | **Sports** | | www.weei.com/
WFNX 101.7 MHz | **Alternative** | | www.broadcast.com/radio/alternative/WFNX/

Canton
TalkAmerica Radio Network 1 | **Talk Radio** | StreamWorks. | www.talkamerica.com/
TalkAmerica Radio Network 2 | **Talk Radio** | StreamWorks. | www.talkamerica.com/

Gloucester
WBOQ "WBACH" 104.9 MHz | **Classical** | | www.wbach.com/getreal.html

Natick
WJLT "J-Light" 1060 kHz | **Christian** | | www.jlight.com/jlitaudio.html

Northampton
WHMP 1400 kHz | **Talk Radio** | NetShow. | www.broadcast.com/radio/talk/WHMP/

100   PASSPORT TO WEB RADIO

Springfield			
WPKX "KIX" 97.9 MHz	Country	NetShow.	www.broadcast.com/radio/Country/WPKX/
Turners Falls			
WPVQ 93.9 MHz	Country		www.wpvq.com/
Worcester			
WAAF 107.3 MHz	Rock	NetShow.	www.broadcast.com/radio/rock/waaf/
Michigan			
Ann Arbor			
WTKA 1050 kHz	Sports	Click "IAS.NET live..."	www.ias.net/goblue/
Dearborn			
WYUR "Your Radio" 1310 kHz	Pop		www.1310.com/
Detroit			
WDFN 1130 kHz	Sports		www.broadcast.com/radio/Sports/WDFN/
WJR 760 kHz	News/Talk/Sports	NetShow.	www.760wjr.com/
WPLT "The Planet" 96.3 MHz	Rock	NetShow.	www.audiolounge.com/stream/providers/wplt/
WRIF 101.1 MHz	Rock	Direct URL:	www.wrif.com/realmedia/wriflive.ram
East Lansing			
WDBM "The Impact" 88.9 MHz	Alternative	Michigan State Univ.	www.wdbm.msu.edu/Listen.html
Houghton			
WMTU 91.9 MHz	College Radio	Michigan Tech. U.	wmtu.resnet.mtu.edu/
Howell			
WHMI 93.5 MHz	Rock		www.whmi.com/require.html
Kalamazoo			
WKZO 590 kHz	News Talk	On demand site.	www.kazoobiz.com/information/news.htm
Lansing			
WJXQ "Q106" 106.1 MHz	Rock		www.broadcast.com/radio/Rock/WJXQ/
WXIK "Country Kicks" 94.1 MHz	Country		www.broadcast.com/radio/Country/WXIK/
Manistique			
WTIQ 1490 kHz	Oldies		www.wtiq.com/

Joe Dumars of the Detroit Pistons speaks out over Michigan's superpower WJR-AM.

Michigan State University's WDBM-FM is completely handicapped-accessible. Its studio includes braille-equipped mixing consoles designed and installed for use with wheelchairs.

Marquette			
WUPX 91.5 MHz	Alternative	Northern Michigan U.	www-student.nmu.edu/orgs/wupx/main.html
Monroe			
WTWR 98.3 MHz	Rock		www.tower98.com/html/hear_tower.html
Saginaw			
WTCF 100.5 MHz	Rock	Not 24 hours.	www.100.5thefox.com/
Saint Johns			
WWDX "Edge" 92.1 MHz	Alternative/Talk		www.broadcast.com/radio/alternative/WWDX/
Saint Louis			
WMLM 1520 kHz	Country	Not 24 hours.	www.wmlm.com/
Troy			
IBMC "The Rodeo"	Country		www.theibc.com/rodeo_main.htm
IMBC "The Cafe"	Alternative		www.theibc.com/Cafe_Main.htm
Ypsilanti			
WEMU 89.1 MHz	Sports	Eastern Michigan U. Eagles.	www.wemu.org/realaudio.html

Minnesota

Bemidji			
KBSB "FM90" 89.7 MHz	Alternative	Bemidji State Univ.	www.fm90.org/live/
Grand Rapids			
KAXE 91.7 MHz	Variety		www.kaxe.org/
Hibbing			
KADU 90.1 MHz	Christian Rock		www.kadu.org/
Minneapolis			
A Prairie Home Companion	Weekly Feature	Two hours per week.	phc.mpr.org/netcast/index.cgi
KDWB 101.3 MHz	Top 40	StreamWorks.	www.kdwb.com/kdwblive/index.html
KFAN 1130 kHz	Sports		www.kfan.com/MAIN.html
KMJZ 104.1 MHz	Smooth Jazz	StreamWorks.	www.kmjz.com/live.html
KQRS 92.5 MHz	Rock	NetShow.	www.92kqrs.com/live.html

KSTP 1500 kHz	News Talk		www.am1500.com/
KXXR "93X" 93.7 MHz	Rock	NetShow.	www.93x.com/live.html
NetRadio Café Jazz	Jazz		www.netradio.net/jazz/
NetRadio Classical	Classical		www.netradio.net/classical/
NetRadio Club Groove	Dance & Urban		www.netradio.net/clubgroove/
NetRadio Country	Country		www.netradio.net/country/
NetRadio Earthbeat	World Music		www.netradio.net/earthbeat/
NetRadio Electronica	Electronica		www.netradio.net/electronica/
NetRadio Holiday Music	Holiday Music		www.netradio.net/holiday/
NetRadio KidzRadio	Kids' Radio		www.netradio.net/kidzradio/
NetRadio Modern Rock	Modern Rock		www.netradio.net/modernrock/
NetRadio NetShow Studio	Variety	NetShow.	www.netradio.net/netshow/
NetRadio New Age	New Age		www.netradio.net/newage/
NetRadio Pop Hits	Pop Hits		www.netradio.net/hits/
NetRadio Vintage Rock	Vintage Rock		www.netradio.net/vintagerock/

Mississippi

Clinton
WHJT 93.5 MHz — Contem. Christian — www.mc.edu/whjt/live.html

Jackson
WKTF 95.5 MHz — Country — www.katfish95.com/audio.html

Lumberton
WLNF "Live 95" 95.3 MHz — Adult Contemp. — www.live95fm.com/notes.htm

New Albany
WWKZ 103.5 MHz — Rock — www.kz103.com/

Oxford
WQLJ 93.7 MHz — Rock — www.wqlj.com/

Vickburg
WSTZ 106.7 MHz — Rock — www.z106.com/audio.html

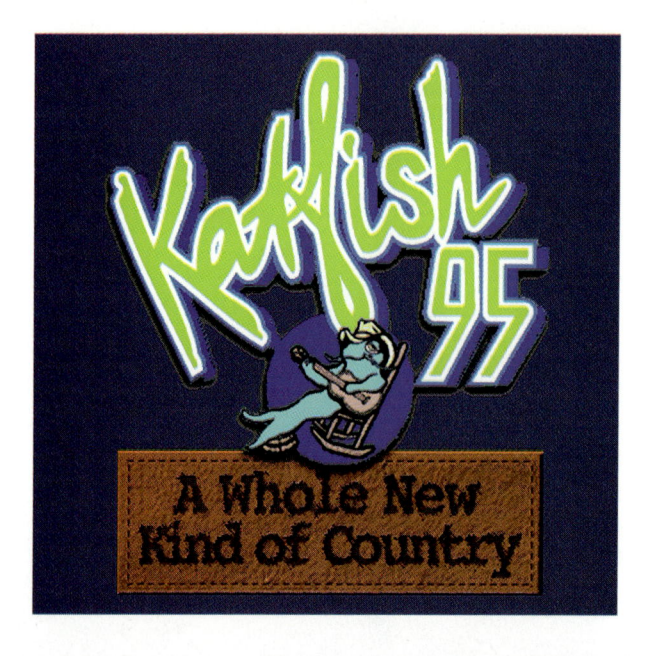

You can't get much more down-home than Jackson, Mississippi, where WKTF-FM airs country music to an appreciative local audience. Now it's on Web radio, so it can be enjoyed everywhere.

The husband-and-wife team of Jim Althoff and Andee Beck are among the personalities providing news and entertainment from St. Louis' KTRS-AM.

Missouri

Kansas City
KCHZ 95.7 MHz	New Rock	www.channelz95.com/z95/asp/real.asp
KCMO 810 kHz	Talk Radio	www.broadcast.com/radio/Talk/KCMO/
KMBZ 980 kHz	News	www.broadcast.com/radio/News/KMBZ/
KOZN "The Zone" 102.1 MHz	Alternative	www.102thezone.com/

Malden
KMAL 92.9 MHz	Rock	www.kmal.com/

Rolla
KMNR 89.7 MHz	Freeform	U. of Missouri. Testing.	www.umr.edu/~kmnr/raudio/

St. Louis
KDHX 88.1 MHz	Eclectic Variety	StreamWorks.	www.kdhxfm88.org/live.asp
KSHE 94.7 MHz	Classic/New Rock		www.kshe95.com/main.html
KTRS 550 kHz	News Talk		www.550ktrs.com/
KXOK "Mix" 97.1 MHz	Urban		www.kxok.com/

Springfield
KTLQ 96.5 MHz	Country	www.broadcast.com/radio/country/kltq/
KTTS-AM 1260 kHz	Classic Country	www.broadcast.com/radio/country/kttsam/
KTTS-FM 94.7 MHz	Country	www.broadcast.com/radio/country/kttsfm/
KTXR 101.3 MHz	Soft Rock	www.ktxrfm.com/

Montana

Kalispell
KOFI-AM 1180 kHz	News Talk	www.marsweb.com/kofi/

Missoula
KBGA 89.9 MHz	Alternative	Click center of page.	kbga.org/
KMSO "Mountain FM" 102.5 MHz	Hits & Favorites	Click on "Listen".	www.kmso.com/
Voice of the Grizzlies	Grizzlies Sports	Univ. of Montana.	www.mtgriz.com/

Although there are few Web stations in New Jersey, each provides a different format. Dover's WDHA excels in contemporary rock.

Nevada
Boulder City
KOOL 105.5 MHz — Oldies — vegasradio.com/kool.html

Incline Village
International News & Broadcasting — News — Click on the **Farsi** button. — www.inbc-news.com/radio/index.htm

Las Vegas
KDWN "K-DAWN" 720 kHz — Talk Radio — www.broadcast.com/radio/Talk/KDWN/

Nebraska
Crete
KDNE "The Kidney" 91.9 MHz — Variety — Doane College. Not 24 hours. — webcast.doane.edu/realaudio.htm

Omaha
WOW-AM 590 kHz — Country — www.broadcast.com/radio/country/wowam/
WOW-FM 94.1 MHz — Country — www.broadcast.com/radio/country/wowfm/

New Hampshire
New London
WNTK 1020 kHz/99.7 MHz — Talk Radio — www.wntk.com/audio/

New Jersey
Dover
WDHA 105.5 MHz — Rock — www.wdhafm.com/

Hackettstown
WNTI 91.9 MHz — Freeform — Centenary College. — www.wnti.org/index2.html

Keansburg
Omega Radio Network — Rock/Miscellany — www.orn.com/

Newark
WBGO 88.3 MHz — Jazz — Click on the radio. — data.jazzcentralstation.com/wbgo/index.asp

New Mexico
Albuquerque
KKSS "Kiss FM" 97.3 MHz — Top 40 — www.broadcast.com/radio/top_40/KKSS/
KLYT 88.3 MHz — Religion — www.thegospel.com/cntidx.htm
KNKT 107.1 MHz — Religion — www.thegospel.com/cntidx.htm

Roswell
KBCQ "Hot 97" 97.1 MHz — Hits — Click on flying saucer. — www.kbcq.com/

Santa Fe
KBAC 98.1 MHz | **Alternative** | Select "Spinning Now". | www.kbac.com/

Taos
KTAO 101.5 MHz | **Alternative** | Select "Spinning Now". | www.ktao.com/

New York
Albany
WAMC 90.3 MHz | **Features** | | www.broadcast.com/radio/archives/wamc/
WAMC 90.3 MHz | **Public Radio** | Not 24 hours. | www.wamc.org/WAMC8.html
WGNA 107.7 MHz | **Country** | NetShow. | www.broadcast.com/radio/Country/WGNA/
WPYX "PYX 106" 106.5 MHz | **Rock** | NetShow. | www.broadcast.com/radio/Rock/WPYX/
WQBK 103.9 MHz | **Alternative** | | www.broadcast.com/radio/alternative/WQBK/

Auburn
WHCD "Smooth FM" 106.9 MHz | **Smooth Jazz** | | www.broadcast.com/radio/Jazz/WHCD/

Briarcliff Manor
WWXY "Y-107" 107.1 MHz | **New Country** | NetShow. | www.newcountryy107.com/

Buffalo
WGR "News Radio 55" 550 kHz | **Sports/News Talk** | | www.broadcast.com/radio/Sports/WGR/
WRUB 770 kHz | **College Radio** | University of Buffalo. | wings.buffalo.edu/ind/sbi/wrub/listen.html

Garden City, L.I.
WLIR 92.7 MHz | **New Rock** | | www.wlir.com/home.htm

Ithaca
WICB "106-VIC" 91.7 MHz | **Rock** | Ithaca College. | www.ithaca.edu/radio/vic/realaudio.htm

Monticello
WJUX "JukeBox Radio" 99.7 | **Big Band/Dance** | | www.broadcast.com/radio/Classics/WJUX/

New York
ABC News | **Hourly news** | Weekday news updates. | www.abcnews.com/
A.P. Network | **News** | On demand bulletins. | audio.nytimes.com/aponline/
CBS News Up To The Minute | **Recent Features** | | uttm.com/whatsnew.html
CBS Radio | **News clips** | | www.cbsradio.com/
CBS Sportsline Audio | **Sports** | 30-day free trial offer. | www.sportsline.com/u/radio/live/sports/index.html
GRIT Internet Broadcasting | **Talk Radio** | | www.grit.net/listen.asp
TBN | **Features** | Chinese. On demand. | tbn.twnet.com/
WABC 770 kHz | **News Talk/Sports** | NetShow. | www.audioactive.com/listen/providers/wabc/

WBBR 1130 kHz	Business News		www.bloomberg.com/wbbr/index.html
WBLS 107.5 MHz	Inner City		www.wbls.com/
WFMU 91.1 MHz	Freeform		www.broadcast.com/radio/Public/WFMU/
WFSH "Fresh 106"	Party Music	On demand site.	www.fresh106.com/
WHTZ "Z100" 100.3 MHz	Hits	NetShow.	www.audioactive.com/listen/providers/whtz/
WLIB 1190 kHz	Inner City		www.wlib.com/index.html
WOR 710 kHz	Talk Radio		www.broadcast.com/radio/Talk/WOR/
WPLJ 95.5 MHz	Classic Hits	NetShow.	www.plj.com/studio/netshow.cfm
WQXR 96.3 MHz	Classical		www.classicalinsites.com/live/wqxr

Plattsburg
WIRY 1340 kHz	Variety		www.wiry.com/
WBTZ "Buzz" 99.9 MHz	Alternative		www.broadcast.com/radio/alternative/wbtz/

Rochester
WBER 90.5 MHz	Modern Rock		wber.monroe.edu/listen.html

Rotterdam
WTRY 98.3 MHz	Oldies	NetShow.	www.broadcast.com/radio/Oldies/WTRY/

Sag Harbor, L.I.
WLNG 92.1 MHz	Oldies		www.wlng.com/

Schenectady
WRUC 89.7 MHz	College Radio	Union College.	www.vu.union.edu/~wruc/

Staten Island, N.Y.C.
WSIA 88.9 MHz	Freeform	Coll. of Staten Island.	wsia.csi.cuny.edu/

Stony Brook, L.I.
WUSB 90.1 MHz	Freeform	State Univ. of N.Y.	www.wusb.org/hear_us.shtml

Syracuse
WHEN 620 kHz	Sports	Subject to blackouts.	www.broadcast.com/radio/sports/WHEN/
WNTQ 93.1 MHz	Hit Rock		www.93q.com/93qreal.html
WSYR 570 kHz	Talk Radio		www.broadcast.com/radio/Talk/WSYR/

Troy
| WRPI 91.5 MHz | **Alternative** | Rensselaer Polytechnic. | www.wrpi.org/ |

North Carolina

Chapel Hill
| WXYC 89.3 MHz | **College Radio** | UNC-Chapel Hill. | www.wxyc.com/ |

Charlotte
Red de Radiodifusión Bíblica	**Christian**	Spanish.	www.worthwhile.com/rrb/
WFNZ 610 kHz	**Sports**		www.broadcast.com/radio/sports/wfnz/
WLNK-FM "The Link" 107.9 MHz	**Rock**		www.1079thelink.com/live.htm
WRFX "Fox" 99.7 MHz	**Classic Rock**		www.broadcast.com/radio/classic_rock/WRFX/
WXRC "Deep Cuts" 95.7 MHz	**Album**		www.broadcast.com/radio/adult_album_alternative/WXRC/

Cullowhee
| WWCU 90.5 MHz | **Hits/Mix** | Western Carolina U. | www.z91.com/listen/index.html |

Durham
| WFXC "Foxy" 107.1 MHz | **Urban** | | www.broadcast.com/radio/Urban/WFXC/ |

Elizabethtown
| WGQR 105.7 MHz | **Oldies** | NetShow. | www.wgqr1057.com/aircheck.htm |

Greensboro
WHSL "Whistle 100" 100.3 MHz	**Country**	NetShow.	www.broadcast.com/radio/country/whsl/
WMAG 99.5 MHz	**Soft Rock**	NetShow.	
WMFR 1230 kHz	**News Talk/Sports**	NetShow.	www.broadcast.com/radio/talk/wmfr/
WNAA 90.1 MHz	**Soul/Urban**	N.C. Agr. & Tech. State U.	drum.ncat.edu/~wnaa/
WTCK "The Ticket" 1320 kHz	**Sports**	NetShow. Off-air sound.	www.broadcast.com/radio/sports/WTCK/

Greenville
| WCBZ "Hot FM" 103.7 MHz | **Hits** | | www.broadcast.com/radio/Contemporary_Hits/WCBZ/ |

Hickory
| WLYT 102.9 MHz | **Adult Contemp.** | NetShow. | www.broadcast.com/radio/adult_contemporary/WLYT/ |

Newport
| Fundamental Broadcasting Network | **Christian** | Grace Missionary Baptist. | www.worthwhile.com/fbn/ |

Pisgah Forest
| WGCR 720 kHz | **Religion** | | www.wgcr.org/ |

Raleigh
Duke Sports Online	**Duke Univ. Sports**		www.dukesports.com/
NC State University Capitol Sports	**NC Sports**		199.72.8.158/broadcasts/capitolnet.html
WDCG 105.1 MHz	**Top 40**	NetShow.	www.broadcast.com/radio/Top_40/WDCG/
WRAL "MIX" 101.5 MHz	**Album**	NetShow.	www.wralfm.com/sound.html
WRDU 106.1 MHz	**Classic Rock**	NetShow.	www.broadcast.com/radio/Classic_Rock/WRDU/
WRSN 93.9 MHz	**Adult Contemp.**		www.broadcast.com/radio/adult_contemporary/WRSN/
WTRG 100.7 MHz	**Oldies**	NetShow.	www.broadcast.com/radio/Oldies/WTRG/

Statesville
| WKKT 96.9 MHz | **Country** | NetShow. | www.broadcast.com/radio/country/WKKT/ |

Washington
| WERO "The Arrow" 93.3 MHz | **Adult Contemp.** | | www.thearrow.com/ |

Wilson
WAHD "Radio Destiny" 90.5 MHz | Smooth Jazz | Requires download of Destiny software. | www.nc.ndl.net/~wahdfm/wahd01.html

Winston-Salem
WSJS 600 kHz | Talk Radio | | www.broadcast.com/radio/Talk/WSJS/
WTOB 1380 kHz | News & Info | Not 24 hours. | www.wtob.com/live.html

North Dakota
Bismarck
KFYR 550 kHz | News Talk | | www.kfyr.com/kfyrlive.htm

Fargo
KFGO "The Mighty" 790 kHz | News/Sports | | www.fargoweb.com/kfgo/audio/index.html

Grand Forks
KCNN 1590 kHz | Sports | | sioux.net/

Ohio
Akron
WKDD 96.5 MHz | Hits | | www.wkdd.com:/wkdd/real.htm

Ashtabula
WZOO 102.5 MHz | Adult Contemp. | | www.knownet.net/wzoo.htm

Belpre
WNUS "US107" 107.1 MHz | Country | NetShow. | www.wnus.com/

Canton
WRQK "Rock 107" 106.9 MHz | Rock | | www.wrqk.com/
WRQK 106.9 MHz | Rock | | www.wrqk.com/

Chardon
WATJ 1560 kHz | Oldies | | www.broadcast.com/radio/oldtime/WATJ/

Cincinnati
WGRR 103.5 MHz | Oldies | | www.wgrr1035.com/liveaudio.htm

Cleveland
WCLV 95.5 MHz | Classical/Religion | Cleveland Lutheran R. NetShow. | www.wclv.com/audio/
WCSB 89.3 MHz | Community Radio | Cleveland State Univ. AudioActive. | www.wcsb.org/
WMJI 105.7 MHz | Oldies | AudioActive. | www.wmji.com/

Coal Grove
WBVB "B97" 97.1 MHZ. | Oldies | | www.wbvb.com/bar.htm

Columbus
KBUX "The Underground" 91.1 MHz | Eclectic | Ohio State University. | kbux.ohio-state.edu/real.html
WCOL 92.3 MHz | Country Favorites | | www.wcol.com/shaudio.html
WLVQ 96.3 MHz | Rock | Click on the loudspeaker. | www.qfm96.com/home.html
WLYR 107.9 MHz | Lite Rock | | www.wlyr.com/
WUFM "Radio U" 88.7 MHz | Christian Rock | | www.radiou.com/real.html

Dayton
WBTT "The Beat" 94.5 MHz | Urban | | www.broadcast.com/radio/Urban/WBTT/
WGNZ 1110 kHz | Southern Gospel | | www.good-news.org/
WGXM "Flyer Radio" 98.1 MHz | Rock/Sports | University of Dayton. | www.udayton.edu/~flyer-radio/live.htm
WHIO 1290 kHz | News Talk/Sports | | drew.broadcast.com/schools/Dayton/index.html

Remember what country was like before it sounded like pop? That's what it still is at Portsmouth, Ohio's WNXT-AM, honky-tonkying worldwide at www.wnxt.com/classic.htm.

WLQT "Lite" 99.9 MHz	Adult Contemp.		www.broadcast.com/radio/Adult_Contemporary/WLQT/
WMMX "Mix" 107.7 MHz	Adult Contemp.		www.broadcast.com/radio/adult_contemporary/wmmx/
WONE "Star 98" 980 kHz	Classic Pop		www.broadcast.com/radio/Classics/WONE/
WTUE 104.7 MHz	Rock		www.broadcast.com/radio/Rock/WTUE/
WXEG "The Edge" 103.9 MHz	Alternative		www.broadcast.com/radio/alternative/WXEG/

Delphos
WDOH 107.1 MHz — Country — www.im3.com/wdoh.htm

Fredericktown
WWBK-98.3/WBZW-107.7 MHz — Country — www.kcountry.com/raudio.htm

Gahanna
WCVO 104.9 MHz — Christian — www.wcvo.com/

Geneva
WKKY 104.7 MHz — Country — www.broadcast.com/radio/Country/WKKY/

Kent
WKSU-FM 89.7 MHz — Classical/College — StreamWorks+RA — www.wksu.kent.edu/live/

Lancaster
WHOK 95.5 — Country — www.whok.com/k95live.html

Liberty Township
Free Radio 1055 — Christian Rock — www.freeradiofreerock.com/

Niles
WNCD 106.1 MHz — Classic Rock — www.cd106.com/

Portsmouth
WNXT 1260 kHz — Classic Country — www.wnxt.com/class.htm
WNXT-FM "The X" 99.3 MHz — Rock — www.wnxt.com/thex.htm

South Webster
WZIO "The Comet" 94.9 MHz — All '70s — www.zoomnet.net/~wzio/jukebox/playlist.html

Toledo
TURADYO — Turkish Songs — Turkish. — www.turkiye.org/radyo/

Oklahoma

Bethany
KNTL 104.9 MHz — Sports Talk — www.sportstalk1049.com/

Claremore
KRSC 91.3 MHz — Rock — Rogers University. — www.rogersu.edu/krsc/radio/

Oklahoma City
KATT "The Cat" 100.5 MHz — Rock — www.broadcast.com/radio/rock/katt/
KYIS "Kiss" 98.9 MHz — Adult Contemp. — www.broadcast.com/radio/adult_contemporary/kyis/

Jim White relaxes at a listener appreciation party for SportsTalk Radio KNTL in Bethany, Oklahoma.

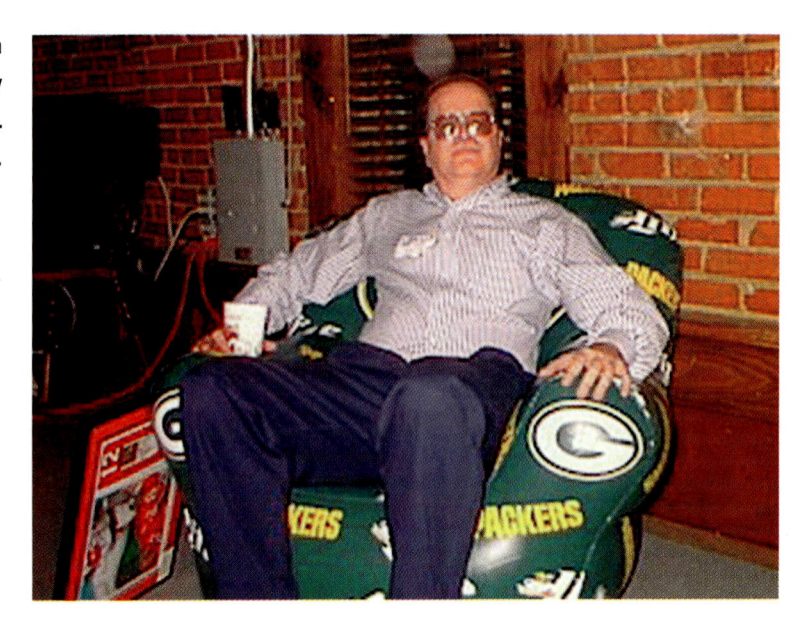

KOCC 88.9 MHz	"Positive Radio"	Oklahoma Christian U.	www.oc.edu/pr89/
KTNT 97.9 MHz	Smooth Jazz		www.ktnt.com/
Pulse 22.5	Favorites		www.pulsemusic.com/

Tulsa
Gospel Media Network	Christian Talk	www.gospelmedia.com/
KCKI 99.5 MHz	Country	www.broadcast.com/radio/country/KCKI/
KVOO 98.6 MHz	Country	www.broadcast.com/radio/country/KVOO/

Oregon
Florence
KCST 1250 kHz/106.9 MHz	Standards	www.presys.com/kcst/audio.html

Medford
KCNA 97.7/102.7 MHz	Oldies	www.kcna.com/listen.htm

Oregon City
KFXX "The FAN" 1520 kHz	Sports	www.broadcast.com/radio/Sports/KFXX/

Portland
KBNP 1410 kHz	Business	www.broadcast.com/radio/business/kbnp/index.html
KGON 92.3 MHz	Classic Rock	www.broadcast.com/radio/classic_rock/KGON/
KNRK "New Rock" 94.7 MHz	Alternative	www.broadcast.com/radio/Alternative/KNRK/
KXL 750 kHz	News	www.pacificharbor.com/kxl/

Pennsylvania
Bethlehem
WZZO 95.1 MHz	Classic & New Rock	www.wzzo.com/

Erie
WFGO "Froggy 94" 94.7 MHz	Oldies	www.froggy-94.com/
WJET 102.3 MHz	Hits	www.jet102.com/

Harrisburg
WWKL 99.3 MHz	Oldies	www.broadcast.com/radio/oldies/WWKL/

VOICES FROM HOME 111

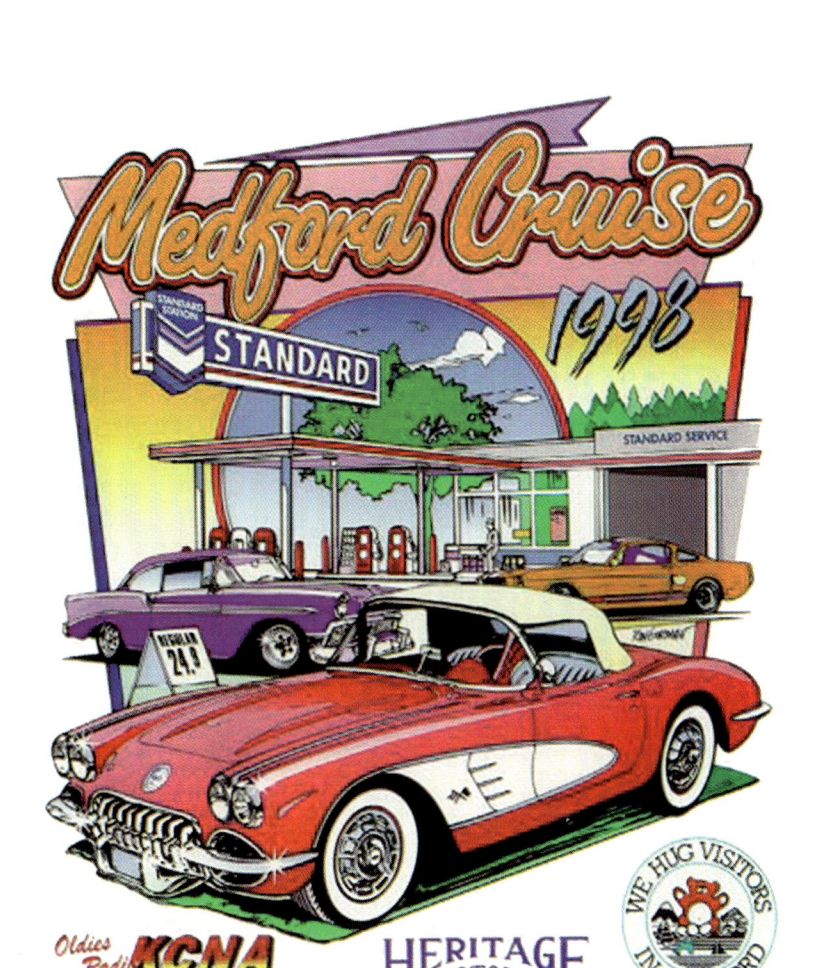

For music that fits in with the cars and gas prices, try KCNA, oldies FM in Medford, Oregon. It's the most!

Lancaster			
WLAN 96.9 MHz	Rock		www.fm97.com/fm97menu.html
Media			
WPLY 100.3 MHz	New Rock		www.y100.com/
Philadelphia			
WHYY 90.9 MHz	**Talk/Features**	Subject to blackouts.	whyy.org/91FM/live.html
WXXM "Max" 95.7 MHz	**Adult Contemp.**		www.broadcast.com/radio/adult_contemporary/WXXM/
Philipsburg			
WPHB 1260 kHz	**Country**	Poor off-air audio.	www.thecampus.com/wphb/
WUBZ 105.9 MHz	**New Rock**		buzzfm.srt.net/
Pittsburgh			
Ann On-line	**Talk/Interviews**	On demand site.	www.annonline.com/
KQV 1410 kHz	**News/Talk/Sports**		www.triblive.com/kqv/
WDRV "The River" 96.1 MHz	**Modern Hits**	NetShow.	www.broadcast.com/radio/adult_contemporary/wdrv/
WDVE 102.5 MHz	**Rock**	NetShow.	www.broadcast.com/radio/rock/wdve/

Pittsburgh's nonprofit WQED provides some of the finest classical music in the world, and it's ad-free.

WJJJ 104.7 MHz	Smooth Jazz	NetShow.	www.broadcast.com/radio/jazz/wjjj/
WPTS 92.1 MHz	Freeform	Univ. of Pittsburgh.	www.wpts.pitt.edu/realaudio/
WQED 89.3 MHz	Classical		www.wqed.org/fm/index.html
WRCT 88.3 MHz	Freeform	Carnegie Mellon U. AudioActive.	www.wrct.org/
WTAE 1250 kHz	Sports		www.broadcast.com/radio/Sports/WTAE
WRRK 96.9 MHz	Classic Rock		www.rrk.com/
WXDX "The X" 105.9 MHz	New Rock	NetShow.	www.broadcast.com/radio/alternative/wxdx

Scranton
WEZX "Rock 107" 106.9 MHz	Rock 'n' Roll		www.rock107.com/

State College
WINK 107.9 MHz	Rock		www.thecampus.com/wink/
WQWK 97.1 MHz	Rock		www.thecampus.com/qwkrock/
WRSC 1390 kHz	Sports		www.thecampus.com/wrsc/

Rhode Island
Bristol
WQRI 88.3 MHz	Rock	Roger Williams Univ.	wqri.dyn.ml.org/real.html

Providence
WBRU 95.5 MHz	Modern Rock		wbru.com/

South Carolina
Gaffney
WYFG 91.1 MHz	Christian	Bible Broadcasting Net.	www.worthwhile.com/bbn/

Greenville
WLFJ 89.3 MHz	Christian		www.hisradio.org/realaudio.htm
WMUU 94.5 MHz	MOR/Religion		www.worthwhile.com/wmuu/

Spartanburg
WORD 910 kHz | **News Talk** | Not 24 hours. | www.worthwhile.com/word/default.htm

South Dakota
Rapid City
KKMK "Magic" 93.9 MHz | **Hits** | | www.rapidnet.com/magic/

Yankton
WNAX 570 kHz | **Variety** | | www.wnax.com/ListenLive/

Tennessee
Chattanooga
WGOW 102.3 MHz | **Talk Radio** | Subject to blackouts. | www.broadcast.com/radio/Talk/WGOW/
WGOW 1150 KHz | **News** | | www.broadcast.com/radio/News/WGOW/
WOGT "GT108" 107.9 MHz | **Oldies** | | www.broadcast.com/radio/Oldies/WOGT/
WSKZ "KZ-106" 106.5 MHz | **Classic Rock** | | www.broadcast.com/radio/classic_rock/WSKZ/

Colonial Heights
WRZK 105.9 MHz | **Rock** | | www.wrzk.com/

Columbia
WAYM "WAY FM" 88.7 MHz | **Christian Rock** | | wayfm.com/live/

Dyersburg
WASL "SL100" 100.1 MHz | **All Hits** | | www.wasl.com/live.htm

Etowah
WDRZ "J103" 103.1 MHz | **Contem. Christian** | CCN Hit Radio. | www.j103.com/pages/ccminternet.html

Knoxville
WNOX 990 kHz/99.1 MHz | **News Talk** | Subject to blackouts. | www.newstalk99.com/home.htm

Memphis
WEGR "Rock 103" 102.7 MHz | **Classic Rock** | | www.broadcast.com/radio/classic_rock/WEGR/
WEVL 89.9 MHz | **Eclectic** | Restricted to members. | www.wevl.org/cdpage.html
WHBQ "Sports 56" 560 kHz | **Sports** | | www.broadcast.com/radio/Sports/WHBQ/
WRVR "The River" 104.5 MHz | **Adult Contemp.** | | www.broadcast.com/radio/adult_contemporary/WRVR/
WRXQ "96X" 95.7 MHz | **Alternative** | From Olive Branch, MS. | www.broadcast.com/radio/alternative/WRXQ/
WSFZ "Super Sport" 1030 kHz | **Sports** | Subject to blackouts. | www.broadcast.com/radio/Sports/WSFZ/

Nashville
Bluegrass Radio Network | **Blue Grass clips** | | www.bluegrassradio.com/audio.html
WLAC-AM 1510 kHz | **News/Talk/Sports** | NetShow. | www.broadcast.com/radio/talk/wlacam/

How much more country can you get than Abilene, Texas? Paula ("P.J.") Rowland holds the fort weekday mornings.

WLAC-FM 105.9 MHz	Classic Rock	NetShow.	www.broadcast.com/radio/classic_rock/wlac/
WRLT "Lightning 100" 100.1 MHz WRLT/		Album	www.broadcast.com/radio/adult_album_alternative/
WRVW "The River" 107.5 MHz	Adult Contemp.	NetShow.	www.broadcast.com/radio/adult_contemporary/WRVW/
WSIX 97.9 MHz	Country	NetShow.	www.broadcast.com/radio/Country/WSIX/

Union City
WWUC "The Quake" 105.7 MHz	Rock		www.realrockradio.com/listen2.htm

Texas
Abilene
KACU 89.7 MHz	Classical/Mix	Abilene Christian U.	www.kacu.org/
KEAN 105.1 MHz	Country		keanradio.com/
KEYJ 107.9 MHz	Rock		www.abileneradio.com/
KGNZ 88.1 MHz	Religion		www.kgnz.com/

Amarillo
KACV 89.9 MHz	College Radio	Amarillo College.	www.kacvfm.org/

Arlington
Praise Broadcasting Network	Christian		www.broadcast.com/lightsource/radio/pbn/

Austin
Brainwash	Techno/Progressive		monsterbit.com/brainwash/
KGSR 107.1 MHz	Album		www.broadcast.com/radio/adult_album_alternative/KGSR/
KROX "101X" 101.5 MHz	Alternative		www.broadcast.com/radio/Alternative/KROX/

Balch Springs
KSKY 660 kHz	Christian		www.broadcast.com/radio/Christian/KSKY/

Beaumont
KIOC "Hot 106" 106.1 MHz	Top 40		www.broadcast.com/radio/top_40/KIOC/
KKMY 104.5 MHz	Adult Contemp.		www.broadcast.com/radio/adult_contemporary/KKMY/
KLVI 560 kHz	Talk Radio	Subject to blackouts.	www.broadcast.com/radio/Talk/KLVI/
KOGT 1600 kHz	Sports/Country		www.kogt.com/
KYKR 95.1 MHz	Country		www.broadcast.com/radio/Country/KYKR/

Carthage
KTUX "The Rebel Rocker" 98.9	Rock		www.broadcast.com/radio/rock/KTUX/

College Station
WTAW 1150 kHz	Sports		www.broadcast.com/radio/Sports/WTAW/

Corpus Christi
Palmsradio	Various		www.palmsradio.com/

Dallas
"Cool 106 FM"	Classic Rock		www.broadcast.com/radio/classic_rock/Cool/

"Dance 103 FM"	Dance		www.broadcast.com/radio/Dance/Dance/
"JAZZY 107 FM"	Jazz	NetShow.	www.broadcast.com/radio/internal/asx/jazzy/
"KLASI 100 FM"	Classical	NetShow.	www.broadcast.com/radio/internal/asx/klasi/
"XMAS 101 FM"	Christmas Music	"Christmas—All year".	www.broadcast.com/radio/special_broadcasts/XMAS/
Dead Radio	Grateful Dead		www.deadradio.com/
Eclectic Rock Radio	Classic Rock		www.broadcast.com/radio/classic_rock/Eclectic_Rock/
Floyd Radio	Pink Floyd		www.floydradio.com/
Glossy Radio	Teen Radio	NetShow.	www.broadcast.com/radio/glossy/
HardRadio	Heavy Metal	NetShow+RA.	www.hardradio.com/tune.html
KBFB 97.9 MHz	Adult Contemp.	NetShow.	www.broadcast.com/radio/contemporary/kbfb/
KCBI 90.9 MHz	Christian		www.kcbi.org/index1.html
KDGE "The Edge" 94.5 MHz	Alternative		www.broadcast.com/radio/Alternative/KDGE/
KKDA "K104FM" 104.5 MHz	Urban		www.broadcast.com/radio/Urban/KKDA/
KKZN "The Zone" 93.3 MHz	Album		www.broadcast.com/radio/adult_album_alternative/KKZN/
KLIF 570 kHz	Talk Radio		www.broadcast.com/radio/Talk/KLIF/
KPLX 99.5 MHz	Country		www.broadcast.com/radio/country/KPLX/
KTCK "The Ticket" 1310 kHz	Sports		www.broadcast.com/radio/Sports/KTCK/
KTXQ "Q102" 102.1 MHz	Alternative	NetShow.	www.broadcast.com/radio/alternative/ktxq/
KZPS 92.5 MHz	Classic Rock		www.broadcast.com/radio/classic_rock/KZPS/
Parrot Radio	Jimmy Buffet	NetShow.	www.broadcast.com/radio/internal/parrotradio/
Prime Sports Radio	Sports		www.broadcast.com/radio/Sports/Prime_Sports/
Radio 80's	80's Rock		www.radio80s.com/
rip-off radio	Alternative		www.broadcast.com/shows/thebigrip-off/default.asp?info=radio
RockTime Radio	Rock	NetShow+RA.	www.broadcast.com/radio/internal/asx/rocktime/
Stash Radio	Music of "Phish"		www.phishradio.com/
Texas Flood Radio	Stevie R. Vaughan	NetShow.	www.broadcast.com/radio/internal/asx/texas_flood/
The Blues Summit	Blues	NetShow+RA.	www.broadcast.com/radio/internal/asx/blues_summit/

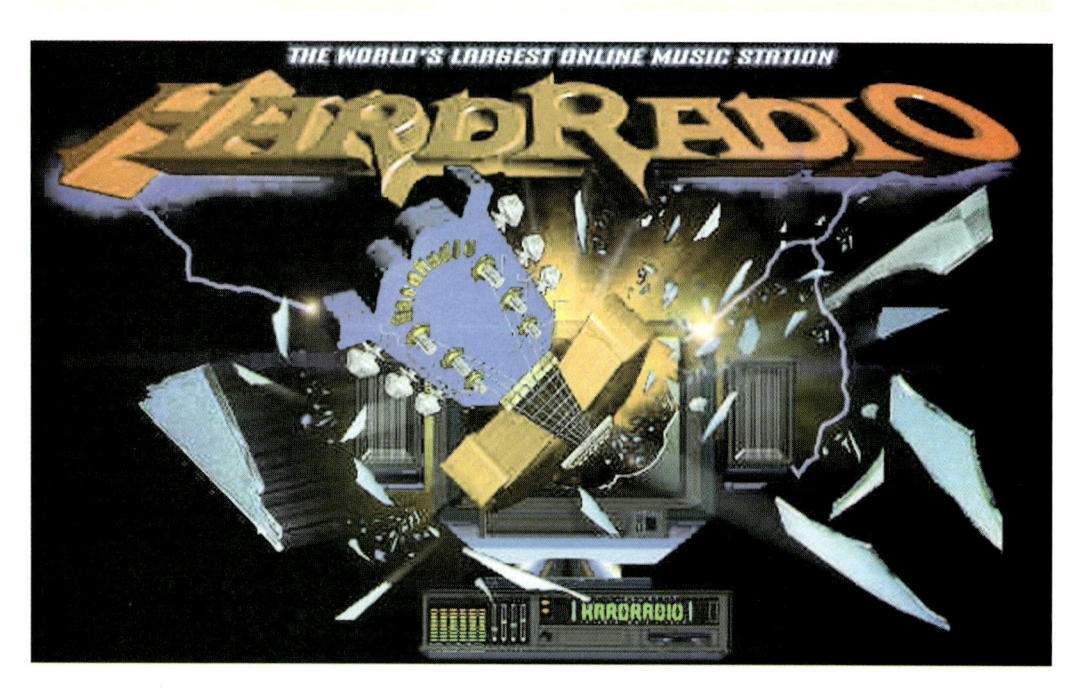

WBAP 820 kHz	News Talk		www.wbap.com/prog-275.html
wRAP.radio	Urban		www.wrapradio.com/
Decatur			
KRNB "Classic RnB" 105.7 MHz	Urban		www.broadcast.com/radio/Urban/KRNB/
Denton			
KHKS "Kiss" 106.1 MHz	Top 40		www.kiddkiss.com/
El Paso			
KATH "Cat Country" 94.7 MHz	Country		www.broadcast.com/radio/country/KATH/
KOFX "The Fox" 92.3 MHz	Oldies		www.broadcast.com/radio/Oldies/KOFX/
KSET 94.7 MHz	Country		www.broadcast.com/radio/country/KSET/
Ft. Worth			
KLTY 94.1 MHz	Contem. Christian		www.audiozoo.com/klty.html
Fresno			
KMJ 580 kHz	Talk Radio		www.broadcast.com/radio/Talk/KMJ/
Houston			
KBXX "The Box" 97.9 MHz	Urban		www.kbxx.com/eventlist.htm
KHCB 105.7 MHz	Religion		www.khcb.org/
KILT "Star 610" 610 kHz	Sports	Not 24 hours.	www.star610kilt.com/
KKPN "The Planet" 102.9 MHz	Adult Contemp.	NetShow.	www.broadcast.com/radio/adult_contemporary/kkpn/
KKRW "The Arrow" 93.7 MHz	Classic Rock	NetShow.	www.broadcast.com/radio/classic_rock/KKRW/
KLOL "K101" 101.1 MHz	Rock	NetShow.	netshow.wl.net/live/klol.htm
KMJQ "Majic" 102.1 MHz	Urban	Click "MAJIC 102 LIVE".	www.kmjq.com/
KODA 99.1 MHz	Adult Contemp.	NetShow.	www.broadcast.com/radio/adult_contemporary/koda/
KPRC "Supertalk" 950 kHz	News Talk	Click on "Station AV".	supertalk.houstonradio.com/menu2.htm
KQUE 1230 kHz	Classic Pop	NetShow.	www.broadcast.com/radio/Classics/KQUE/
KRBE 104.1 MHz	Top 40		www.broadcast.com/radio/top_40/KRBE/
KRTS 92.1 MHz	Classical		www.broadcast.com/radio/Classical/KRTS/
KTBZ "The Buzz" 107.5 MHz	Alternative		www.broadcast.com/radio/Alternative/KTBZ/
World Talk Network, Inc	Business		www.broadcast.com/shows/worldtalk/
Katy			
PowerSource ("KWCJ"/ "KWCM")	Christian Rock		www.kwcm.com/listento.htm

New Boston			
KEWL 95.1 MHz	Oldies		www.broadcast.com/radio/Oldies/KEWL/
Paris			
KOYN 93.9 MHz	Country		www.1starnet.com/koyn/
Plano			
KAAM "Unforgettable" 620 kHz	Pop/Sports		www.broadcast.com/radio/Classics/KAAM/
Port Arthur			
KHYS 98.5 MHz	Urban/New Music		www.khys.com/news-text.htm
Richardson			
Yesterday USA Superstation	Old Time Radio		www.broadcast.com/radio/oldtime/yestrday/
San Antonio			
KCHG 810 kHz	Religion		www.kchg.com/realaudio.htm
KSJL 96.1 MHz	Urban		www.broadcast.com/radio/Urban/KSJL/
WOAI 1200 kHz	Talk Radio	Subject to blackouts.	www.broadcast.com/radio/Talk/WOAI/
San Marcos			
KTSW 89.9 MHz	Diverse	Southwest Texas State Univ.	www.ktsw.swt.edu/Live/
Micro Kind Radio 105.9 MHz	Community Radio		www.mediadesign.net/kindmenu.htm
Seguin			
KWED 1580 kHz	Country		www.kwed1580.com/
Temple			
KTEM 1400 kHz	News Radio		www.ktem.com/
Waco			
KBBW 1010 kHz	Christian		www.kbbw.com/
Willis			
KVST "K-Star" 103.7 MHz	Country		www.broadcast.com/radio/country/kvst/

Utah

Brigham City			
KLZX 106.9 MHz	Rock		klzx.com/
Ogden			
KSOS 800 kHz	Oldies		www.ksos.com/
Provo			
KBYU 89.1 MHz	Classical		www.kbyu.byu.edu/fm/realaudio.html
Salt Lake City			
KFNZ "KFAN" 1320 kHz	Sports		www.broadcast.com/radio/Sports/KFNZ/

KSL 1160 kHz	News Radio	StreamWorks+RA.	www.ksl.com/radio/
KUMT "The Mountain" 105.7 MHz	Adult Contemp.		www.broadcast.com/radio/adult_contemporary/KUMT/
LDS Radio Network	Christian	Bonneville Internat.	www.ldsradio.com/

Vermont

Burlington

WIZN "Wizard of Rock" 106.7 MHz	Rock		www.broadcast.com/radio/rock/wizn/
WRUV 90.1 MHz	Freeform	Univ. of Vermont.	www.uvm.edu/~wruv/

Killington

WEBK "The Mountain" 105.3 MHz	Eclectic Mix		www.webk.com/wlisten.shtml

Monpelier

WNCS 104.7 MHz	Rock		wncs.com/wncs/wncs.htm

Plainfield

WGDR 91.1 MHz	Political Talks		www.goddard.edu/wgdr/audio.html

Randolph Center

WVTC 90.7 MHz	College Radio	Vermont Tech. College AudioActive.	www.wvtc.net/livefeed.html

Woodstock

WMXR "Magic 94" 93.9 MHz	Classic Hits		www.magic94fm.com/audio/

Virginia

Cape Charles

WROX "96X" 96.1 MHz	Rock		www.broadcast.com/radio/rock/wrox/

Chantilly

Christian Community Network	Christian Hits		www.christcom.net/radio/

Fairfax

WEBR 94.5 MHz	Eclectic Variety	Cable station.	www.axsamer.org/webr/listen.html
WGMU 1370 kHz	College Radio	George Mason Univ.	wgmu.gmu.edu/real_audio.html

Norfolk

WKOC "The Coast" 93.7 MHz	Alternative		www.broadcast.com/radio/adult_album_alternative/wkoc/
WNVZ 104.5 MHz	Pop/Rhythm/Hits		www.z104.com/
WODU 640 kHz	Sports	Live sports.	www.odu.edu/~athletic/ra.htm

Keepin' the 70's Alive
3 hours of classic music from the 70's! Sundays 10-1

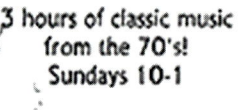

If local classic rock leaves you tuned out, surf among the oodles of great choices on the Web. WMXR-FM in Woodstock, Vermont, airs rock hits from the sixties, seventies and eighties, including one three-hour block of nothing but 1970s cuts.

Morning Show host Brad Eaton and Marketing and Promotion Coordinator Andrea DeCou at KING-FM's live broadcast from the Seattle Art Museum.

Richmond
WSMJ "Smooth Jazz" 101.1 MHz — Jazz — www.wsmj.com/listenlive.htm

Salem
WPAR "PARfm" 91.3 MHz — Christian Hits — www.parfm.com/

Virginia Beach
WPTE "The Point" 94.9 MHz — Rock — www.pointradio.com/

Warrenton
WUPP "Up Country" 94.3 MHz — Country — www.broadcast.com/radio/Country/WUPP/

Washington

Centralia
KITI 95.1 MHz — Rock — www.live95.com/realaudi.htm

Chelan
KOZI 1230 kHz/93.5 MHz — Soft Rock — www.kozi.com/index.html

College Place
KGTS 91.3 MHz — Contem. Christian — Walla Walla College. www.plr.org/audio/

Ellensburg
KCAT 91.5 MHz — Alternative — Central Washington U. www.cwu.edu/~kcat/

Olympia
TVW (Washington St. Public Affairs) — Governmental — www.tvw.org/dayprog.htm

Seattle
KING "Classic KING FM" 98.1 MHz — Classical — www.king.org/content/real_audio_area/index.html

Webcasting controls are tweaked at Walla Walla's KTWY, "Way-FM."

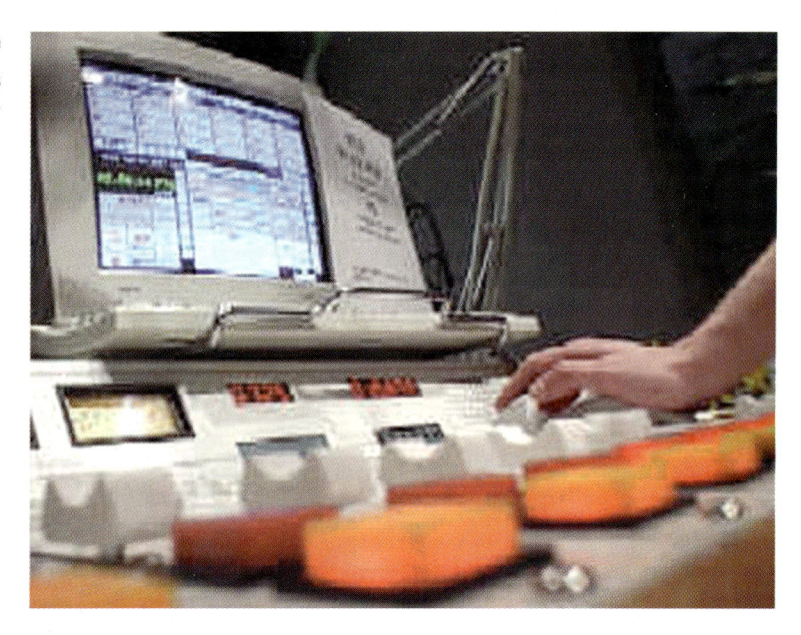

KIRO 710 kHz	News Talk		www.kiro710.com/
KISW 99.9 MHz	Rock	NetShow+RA.	www.kisw.com/kiswlive.html
KJR-AM 950 kHz	Sports	Click on "LISTEN UP!"	www.sportsradio950.com/
KJR-FM 95.7 MHz	Classic Hits	Click "Classic hits live".	www.kjrfm.com/
KMTT 103.7 MHz	Soft Rock		www.kmtt.com/nonframes/newsflash.shtml
KUBE 93.3 MHz	Hits		www.kube93.com/index.html
KYCW 96.5 MHz	Young Country		www.unclewynn.com/yclive.htm
iMusic	Eclectic	*Five* shows on demand.	imusic.com/radio/

Spokane

KGA 1510 kHz	News Talk	Limited live programming.	kga.skywalk.com/radir.html
KSPO 106.5 MHz	Christian Talk	American Christian Network.	www.acn-network.com/
KTRW 970 kHz	Sports	Subject to blackouts.	www.broadcast.com/radio/sports/KTRW/
KXLY-AM 920 kHz	News/Sports	Subject to blackouts.	www.broadcast.com/radio/talk/KXLY/
KXLY-FM "Classy" 99.9 MHz	Soft Hits		www.broadcast.com/radio/adult_contemporary/KXLY/
KZZU "93-Zoo" 92.9 MHz	Top 40		www.broadcast.com/radio/top_40/KZZU/

Vancouver

KFXX "The Fan" 910 kHz	Sports		www.broadcast.com/radio/sports/kfxx/

Walla Walla

KTWY "Way-FM" 93.3 MHz	Christian Hits		www.cradio.net/wayfmh.htm

West Virginia
Charleston

WQBE 97.5 MHz	New Country		www.wqbe.com/index2.html
WVSR "Electric 102" 102.7 MHz	Rock		www.super102.com/newindex/

Elizabeth

WRZZ "Z-106" 106.1 MHz	Classic Rock		classicrockz106.com/livez106.html

Keyser
WQZK 94.1 MHz	Classic Rock	Click the musical notes.	www.wqzk.com/gButton.html

Morgantown
WCLG 100.1 MHz	Rock	Click "Live on the WWW".	www.wclg.com/

Moundsville
WRKP 96.5	Contem. Christian		www.wrkp.com/real.html

Parkersburg
WDMX "Mix 100" 100.1 MHz	Oldies	NetShow.	www.wdmx.com/

Wisconsin

Madison
WSUM 91.7 MHz	College Radio	Univ. of Wisconsin.	msr.wisc.edu/flisten.html

Milwaukee
WISN 1130 kHz	Talk/Sports	NetShow.	www.broadcast.com/radio/talk/WISN/
WLTQ 97.3 MHz	Adult Contemp.	NetShow.	www.broadcast.com/radio/adult_contemporary/WLTQ/
WMUR	Eclectic Mix	Marquette University.	www.mu.edu/stumedia/wmur/index.html
WUMW 89.7 MHz	Features	U. of Wisc.-Milwaukee.	www.uwm.edu/wuwm/soundbytes.html
WVCY "VCY/America" 107.7 MHz	Christian		www.vcyamerica.org/

Wausau
WCLQ 89.5 MHz	Positive Hits		www.89q.org/

Radio Safari is just one of several lively musical features from Victoria FM in Maracay, Venezuela.

Wyoming
Powell
KLZY "Z-92" 92.5 MHz	Rock	www.wir.net/kpowz92/live.htm

VATICAN CITY—Multilingual
Vatican City
Vatican Radio	News	On demand site.	www.wrn.org/vatican-radio/audio.html

VENEZUELA—Spanish
Maracay
Radio Rumbos 88.5 MHz	LA Pop	www.tycom.com.ve/rumbos/la historia.htm
Victoria FM 103.9 MHz	Variety	www.tycom.com.ve/victoria/

VIRGIN ISLANDS—English
Charlotte Am., St. Thomas
WIVI "96 Rock" 96.1 MHz	Rock & Roll	www.96rockwivi.com/

San Jose's "Vietnam FM 96.1" brings news and cultural happenings to the Vietnamese diaspora, as well as haunting Indochinese melodies for everybody to enjoy.

Christiansted, St. Croix
WJKC "Isle 95" 95.1 MHz | Urban | | www.viaccess.net/radio/isle95/index.html

WEST BANK/GAZA—Arabic

Voice of Palestine | **Daily Headlines** | Arabic. | www.bailasan.com/pinc/voice.htm

YUGOSLAVIA—Serbian

Belgrade
Radio B92	**News**	**English**.	www-2.realaudio.com/webactive/events/b92/
Radio B92	**Pop**		www.xs4all.nl/~opennet/
Radio Index 88.9	**Variety**	Off during school holidays.	www.yugoradiopool.co.yu/rindex/rindex.htm
Radio Yugoslavia	**News**	On demand site. Also **English**.	www.beograd.com/radioyu/frconten.htm

VOICE OF PALESTINE

Web Radio's Unexpected Future

by John Campbell

Crystal-ball gazing about the Internet and World Wide Web makes for colorful media copy. Clearly, the legions of trade journalists who churn out these features don't seem to be put off by the old European saying: "All predicting is difficult, especially predicting the future."

The long-term future is the easiest of these futures to handle. After all, a mixture of science fiction and wishful thinking can support almost anything. But how do we get there from here? That depends on the most important features of the situation in 1998—which are not always the most obvious features of what we see and hear on the Internet.

How Did the Web Get Here?

The grandfather of the present Internet was built as a tool for communication, to help American research groups in different places to keep in contact with each other and with the agency that paid their bills. This was not a basic research agency, but an arm of the Pentagon. The development and expansion of what has now become the Internet have been items in the same bills.

Who paid? You did. Or rather we did: we, the taxpayers. It has actually turned out to be a bargain, though we might not have been able to appreciate it during most of the last 30 years, while the development was going on.

The problem is that this kind of financing is now out of fashion. The Pentagon has fewer and smaller enemies than 30 years ago, and therefore much less spare money. And developing the Internet is no longer a research adventure: It has to pay its own way.

The history of the Web is very similar. Just replace "Pentagon" by CERN, a multinational laboratory in Switzerland for basic research in high-energy particle physics, and "American" by "European," and you have it. The European taxpayer paid the bills, but already the formula for this funding is out of date. If CERN had to invent the Web in 1998, there would be a little difficulty: one that caused no real trouble in 1988. Money.

Who Provides the Money in 2001?

In one word, advertisers. Advertising is evidence of commercial activity, and it attracts money from other sources: companies and people who want to sell, developers who want to make money by increasing the volume of Internet business—even governments that want to get in around the edges of the profit-making act.

There is plenty of commerce and development in 1998, but this is mainly speculative. We read stories of businesses actually making profits from Internet and Web commerce now, but finding hard evidence of a positive return on past investment is difficult. Web radio is no exception, as Kim Komando explains elsewhere in this book.

I asked an American Internet guru who had just given an optimistic speech about the future for the Internet recently what would

The author inspects something as rare as good software, a bottle of 1970 Mouton Rothschild from the late baron's private cellar.
Belle E. Heureux

University College London's Website is a key resource for computer professionals. North American access is possible via the University of Southern California's Information Sciences Institute, at north.east.isi.edu/sdr.

happen to this future if the advertising money dried up. First he looked surprised, then horrified. "Never thought of that one before," he said. "It would be disastrous."

Even if the money disappears, surely Web radio in its present form can still survive? Yes, but will the listeners stay with it in its present form? That's easy to answer: maybe no, maybe yes. Web radio in 1998 has some primitive features, but also some good ones that get less praise than they deserve.

"Good Old Radio Days," Revisited

Despite the variety of formats in broadcasting, the number of different perspectives in modern radio is much less than in the good old pioneer days. Basically, every operator now is a broadcasting or media organization. As early American radio magazines like *RADEX* show, things were much more mixed before the mid-1930s. Station operators included automobile and piano dealers, flour milling companies, fraternal orders of woodsmen (whatever these were), and schools of dancing and of theology. Perhaps Grandma Brown's airline and wire door company wasn't in the list, but it must have come close.

We don't have that amount of novelty in Web radio yet. The broadcast.com index classifies stations under the same format headings that wireless broadcasters use among themselves. But the potential of the pioneer days of radio is out there now, waiting to be introduced to the idea of audio via the Internet. The ordinary non-talking sites on the Web already show much more variety than the *RADEX* lists of station operators in the early 1930s. Here is the source material for new directions in the future of Web radio.

Most Websites are dumb—so far. Some offer short canned audio clips, rather like the "talking house" broadcasts on 1610 or 1620 kHz that American real estate agents have used. Radio stations on the Web with both live and on-demand programming are at the other extreme of audio, but it is possible to go even further, in at least two directions at once. First, making the listener into an active participant, with forms of interaction more attractive than those tried to date. Second, combining audio with images.

Yes, images—audio with video doesn't have to be Web TV. That is coming, but not as an outgrowth of Web radio—and anyway, isn't modern TV boring enough on 40+ channels without the need to be bored by 400+ Web channels? Access to exotic foreign material won't add much value. I can report from direct experience that Mongolian TV is every bit as bad as TV in Sioux Falls.

Lomotion Images

There are many possible services where "lomotion" images (graphics, stills, successions of stills, or images in motion for short periods) can enhance greatly what pure audio delivers. Education, home shopping for goods or tourism, and filling out news or features with extra information, are only three of them. The lomotion approach is also appropriate for users who are on the go or otherwise engaged in other activities.

Just think of the difference between your favorite newspaper with and without pictures, and also of how the "with" option could be improved if pictures could be changed while you look at them. For example, "Nice tourist resort you're showing me there, but let's see how crowded the beach is after lunch," or "Wait, that looked interesting, so I'd like you to go back and show it to me again."

Finally, how about having a program of radio and images composed for you automatically, according to your general opinion of what you want, from different Web stations, including those you haven't heard about before? All of these features of "radio plus" are technically possible right now, and in fact are beginning to appear. The pioneering spirit seems to be in good health in Web radio/audio, so we are likely to see many experiments with variations of these ideas, and new ones, in the future. This has to be excellent news for the Web listener.

Problems of Reception

The news from the Web front is not all good, however. The Internet needs to improve before the difficulties and nuisances that it is easy to experience at present can disappear. Some of them are romantic, at least for a short time. They are reminders of the adventure of "DXing" or chasing distant stations in the early days of broadcasting, when you could never know what you were going to hear, or not hear, next. Others are just irritating. And even romantic effects can wear out their welcome quickly.

Here are the most obvious peculiarities in Web DXing:

- interruptions or halts in the audio stream
- complete breaks of service
- difficulty in finding the right link in a site where an audio source is supposed to be
- user-unfriendly and downright user-hostile interfaces
- the http://.... nuisance
- getting what you don't ask for: mainly visual or audio commercials.

In the right futures, fortunately, help will be on hand for each of these. For most of them, we should not have to wait for long.

Ballet of the ISP Elephants

The first two problems in the list come from the biggest bottlenecks in Internet service to the private customer: the telephone system and the bandwidth available at critical points on the network. For somebody who has a dial-up modem, the telephone system is the real villain. It

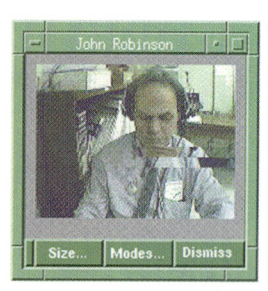

University College London's Website for the *Merci* computer Europroject, also shown on page 129.

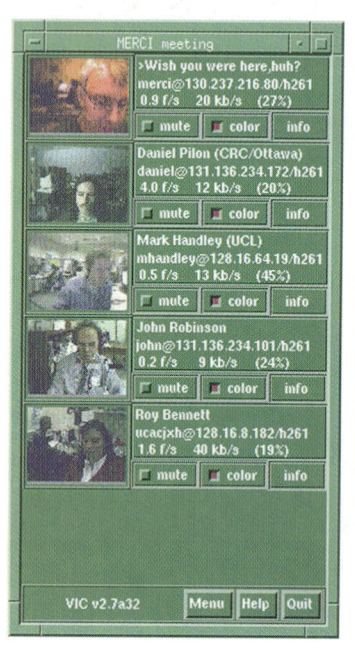

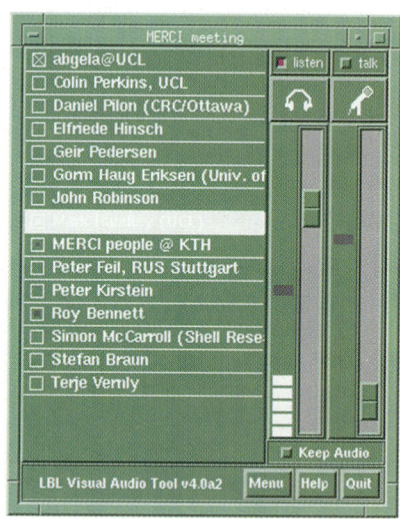

forces early 21st century digital technology to use a 19th century non-digital design to support its service. We need at all costs to avoid talking to the Internet through our 1998-model (sometimes 1898) telephone exchanges.

There are technical ways, like cable modems and ISDN, around this roadblock, but each has its own drawbacks. For example, their bandwidth is currently no better than the low hundreds of kilobits per second, while the networked services of the future will need this to be increased more than ten times. Satellites may be an answer, but if we launch enough of them for a real 21st century global system, we'll have some difficulty seeing the sun during daylight hours. Digital Subscriber Lines (DSLs) or some Internet-friendly improvement are probably the best bet, particularly if and when copper gives way to fiber optics. They don't require large technical advances. Just money.

To predict when all the ingredients will come together in the right way calls for a genius of economics and politics, not technological skill. While the newest small and fast-moving parts of the information technology industry produce and test novel solutions, the older heavy parts are trying to hold onto as much as possible of what they know and love.

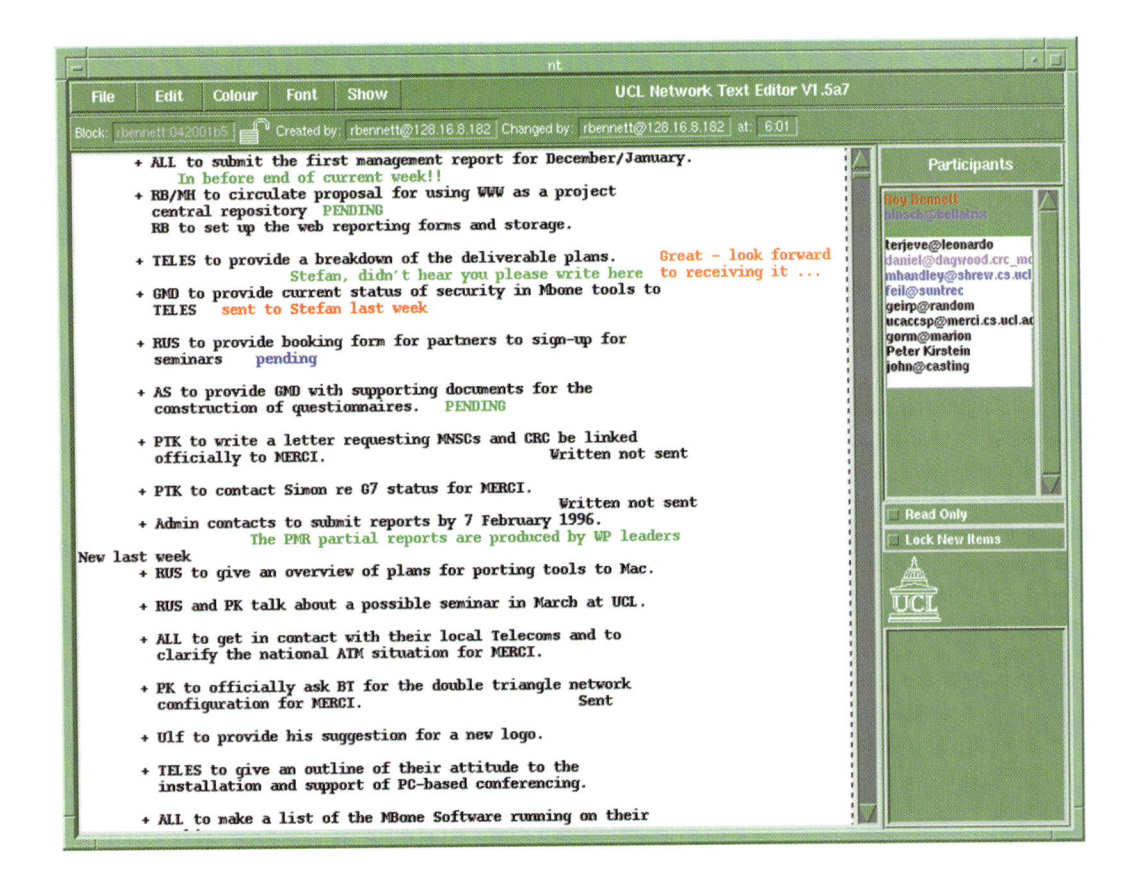

For example, telephone companies may be cautious about modifying their DSL capacity or changing their switching systems to allow digital data to flow faster—let alone developing wireless alternatives that are optimized for networked communication, rather than present-day mobile telephony and modem imitations. Deregulation means that they have to compete, but they prefer to do this by tackling other parties on battlegrounds that are already set up in their favor. When was the last time you saw a genuine head-to-head battle in one American territory between two local telephone companies?

Progress is likely to be slower than the average trade journalist says. The speed will be limited by the heavy end of the industry trying to pry subsidies out of governments without calling them subsidies, and to persuade advertisers to keep on advertising. This ballet of elephants will be fun to watch, especially whenever the telephone company hippopotamuses weigh in to defend their deregulation-powered monopolies.

Luckily, even if the industry doesn't succeed in building a network with multi-megabit bandwidths for all private subscribers, lesser improvements in the capacity of the present Internet structure will mean that we can have reliable Web radio mixed with fresh images—if the application can benefit from it—every few seconds. We can already hear-see this kind of Web radio now. Getting the service reliably is a reasonable target for the next two-to-three years.

Are Bad Interfaces Here to Stay?

No. (This is going to be a short section!) We already know how to build good interfaces and lay out good Web pages to answer the real needs of users. If things are less than perfect at present, this is because some site operators still have five thumbs on each hand. The principles of good ergonomics are widely taught, and should ensure that badly arranged Web access will become less common with time, when information about good practice gets around.

Are Computers Here to Stay?

That depends on where "here" is. If it is your own point of access to the Internet and Web, no.

Personal computers are an historical survival from the pre-Internet period. They fit uneasily with it. Anyone who has struggled with Windows to hunt for information on the Web should have noticed this already. What we need, and what digital commerce needs, is something that is adapted to the structure and behavior of the networks. It may incidentally have or give access to explicit computing for people who want it, but these customers are likely to be in a minority. For the majority, Windows should disappear.

This makes it clearer why Microsoft is exploiting every trick in the book to avoid having to separate its net access software from Windows. In the future, net access will be the primary service for your XXXX, and the sort of computing that operating systems like Windows supports will be an option that most buyers will not use. Microsoft would like to be your favorite software supplier now, then, and during the transition period.

Well, what is your XXXX? Not a "computer." In particular, you should never have to type the likes of http:// again. (This is just an instruction to the computer to perform a particular find-and-retrieve operation on what follows the //). Instead, you will be able to type or say a description of what you are looking for, and the XXXX will ensure that the right knowledge-based computing automatically delivers what you want—including finding that obscure Bolivian Web radio station that a friend told you about last week.

A commercially viable XXXX will have some features of a TV set, and others, like local encryption, that will be required for secure digital commerce. It will be different enough from existing household equipment to justify a new name. If you can register a good XXXX as a trademark, you may be able to retire rich. "Reseo," which is in the same verbal league as audio and video, and comes from the French *reseau*, or network, is a long shot. If it takes off, remember that you heard it here first.

Webman Reseos

Even slow progress in networking can still give us interesting new results in Web radio at our desks or tables. But ordinary radio has long since moved further out into the world: into your automobile, or wherever you want to go. It makes sense for the Web radio customer to demand the same flexibility. What chance do we have that the demand will be answered?

The technology of mobile telephone services goes some way towards doing the job. It needs more bandwidth and a better coverage by local receivers and transmitters, plus some modifications which may not be simple. Here, economics intervenes.

Telephone companies are by far the best placed to make the developments, but they have first to be convinced that the return is worth the investment, that they can have the leading part in writing any new regulations and standards, and that improving this side of their service will not interfere with the profitability of their existing systems. Present indications are confusing; the companies make all the right noises, but the ballet of elephants is lumbering along behind at the same time.

The eventual payoff from any fast motion by the companies is that all the aspects of Web radio that you can hear from your computers will be available in every place where today's Walkman radios can go. Some things, like keyboards, displays of images, and the functions that come with them, may have to stay on your desk, but the rest—including a simple speech interface to make up for the missing keyboard—can already be packaged in small volumes. The potential for expansion of Web radio into a truly mass market through this kind of "Webman" future is enormous. Although it will not happen quickly, mobile Web radio may eventually dominate the stay-at-home kind. Perhaps the ultimate Web predictor was cartoonist Chester Gould, who invented Dick Tracy's wristwatch reseo.

Can We Kill Commercials?

Not if the network operators can help it. We can only hope that clever software will be able to detect and screen out commercials just as VCRs now do, or like anti-virus packages sniff out viruses in programs. Of course, the operators will then try to think up ways to beat the anti-commercial packages. This will keep both sides busy; we third parties should get some benefit from the fighting. But if we block all the commercials, where will the money for Internet and Web development come from? We can't afford to be too clever.

No More Cigars from CBS

Even without a reseo or an XXXX, we can expect the quality and variety of Web radio, near-radio and "radio plus" to improve steadily over at least the next few years. Reception will be more reliable, and from an increasing number of types of station or "station" in more and more countries. Operators will not need professional radio budgets and equipment to give a professional service. Services too will expand: With instant answer-back possible from users, there should be many types of broadcasting or narrowcasting activity besides old-fashioned one-way radio and talk shows. Even the most silent current Website can become vocal with the help of audio technologies.

It is safe to predict that the boundaries between silent sites on the one hand and traditional Web radio on the other will become blurred, sometimes in ways we cannot guess yet. Grandma Brown's airline and wire door company has just as much chance of inventing something new as the most sophisticated Web radio station of the moment. Remember (if you read the radio history books) that CBS started life as a New York business importing Cuban cigars.

John Campbell is professor of computer science at University College London, and a consultant and general animator in European Union programs for multinational R&D in advanced information technologies. He has written many scientific papers on his research in knowledge-based systems, intelligent agents, communications and computer processing of material in multiple languages.

Webcasting: Can It Pay?

by Kim Komando

Webcasting has become the latest buzzword in radio stations across America and around the world. However, as with so many things related to computer technology these days, if you ask a dozen different people to describe Webcasting and all that the word implies, you'll probably get a dozen different answers.

First let's start with a short definition. Webcasting takes programming that would normally be over-the-air, and redirects it through the millions of circuits that make up the Internet. Listeners who connect to the Internet can "tune" to a broadcast by directing their Web browser to a radio station's Web page. Once there, they can listen to the programming.

Three Categories of Webcasting

Web radio programming falls into one of three categories: live, archive and on-demand—a station's overall Webcast content can consist of any combination of these. For example, "Sports Byline USA" airs live sports-talk radio over the Web seven days a week from 10 PM to 6 AM Eastern time. Listeners who tune in outside that time slot hear archived highlights from previous Webcasts.

On-demand simply means giving the listener control over what archived programming they hear. For example, it can be used to offer especially popular or interesting segments from previous shows.

This sounds simple, and on the surface, it is. However, there are plenty of technical considerations to be thought through before a conventional radio station jumps into Webcasting. Thousands of stations now have Websites where listeners can find supplementary information about the station. Delivering these relatively static Web pages is light duty for Web serving systems.

Up-to-Date Systems Needed

On the other hand, if a station is going to Webcast it needs a very powerful and reliable system, including high-speed connection to the Internet. This system has to be capable of pumping out a continuous stream of material to potentially thousands of people at a time. If a station opts for a do-it-yourself approach, it is looking at a considerable investment in both equipment and staff.

Stations also have to consider the technical aspects of listeners' equipment; any old computer won't do. They need fairly up-to-date equipment, including at least a 56 kbps modem to connect to the Internet. Plus, they need special software to interpret and listen to Webcasts.

Just like any static file that's transmitted across the Internet, Webcast programming is delivered in a particular format that can only be processed by the corresponding software on the listener's system. The most popular of these formats is RealAudio, but there are several others in use, including NetShow, Audioactive and

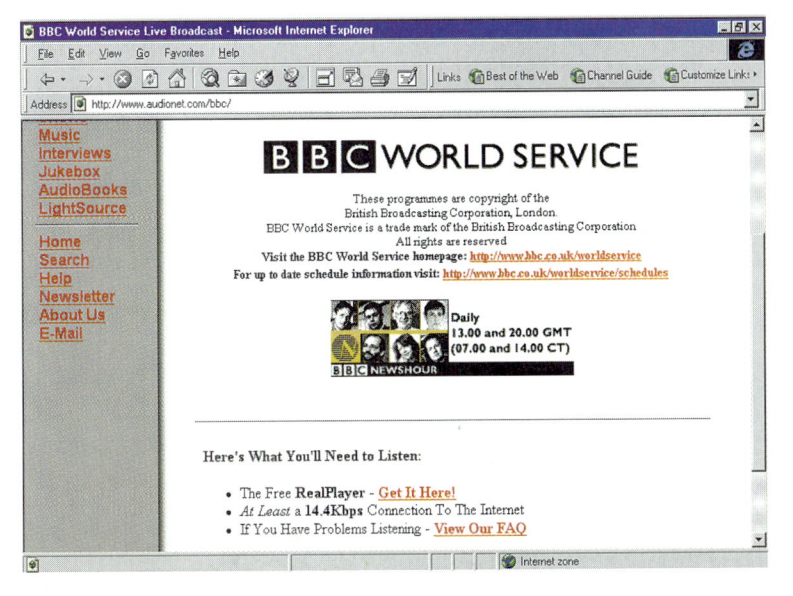

The BBC World Service's Web audio page was one of the most heavily visited Internet sites during Princess Di's funeral. It is also where you can listen to the world's most authoritative international news.

StreamWorks, and all are free. If the listener doesn't have the proper software to listen, stations need to provide an easy means to download it from their site.

Who Listens, and Why

One important question is: What would prompt listeners to go to all the trouble of tuning in to a Webcast rather than just clicking on their radio?

Author Kim Komando hosts a number of shows on radio and television, as well as writing popular newspaper and magazine columns. Her WestStar organization is one of radio's fastest-growing networks, and she was guest speaker on Web radio at NAB '98.

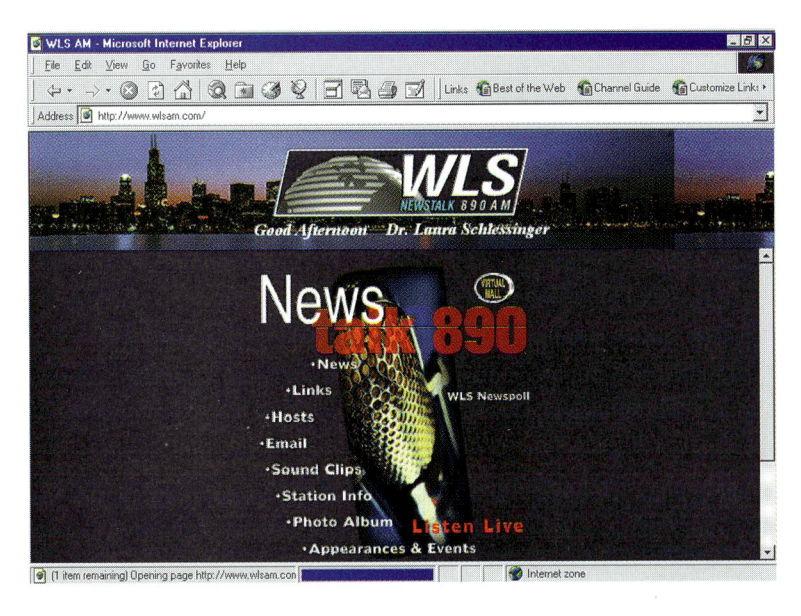

Chicago's "Big 89" is a traditional clear-channel AM powerhouse. Its Web audio is among the best, too.

First, Webcasting allows listeners to tune outside their normal listening area, which expands a station's market from local to worldwide. These distant markets don't have local stations with the quality or formats some listeners want, so Web radio fills the audience gap.

If a station has programming that stands out—strong personalities, creative playlist, local sports events, distinctive format or any sort of universal appeal—listeners around the world can and will tune in, given the proper promotion. Any station thus has the opportunity to reach an audience as large or larger than that of any syndicated programming.

Speaking of syndicated programming, Web stations need to check licensing agreements. In the United States many syndicated programs—from Dr. Laura and Rush Limbaugh to the Metropolitan Opera and many sportscasts—specifically prohibit Webcasting for most stations.

Another ticklish point is that Arbitron, RAJAR, Médiamétrie and other measures of audience size are based on the traditional model of local over-the-air transmissions. This poses a two-fold problem: Who gets the ratings credit, and will the listener even be savvy enough to list the stations and/or program heard on the Web in something like an Arbitron diary?

Say, someone who lives in Seattle is listening to a program on the Web from a station in Atlanta, yet a local Seattle station also carries the same program. Which station gets the credit, or does the credit go to the innocuous Arbitron Internet category? In a worst case scenario, neither the stations nor the syndicated program gets Arbitron credit. In that case, everyone loses.

Clearly, syndicators must keep the delicate balance of servicing and pleasing the local affiliate while, at the same time, doing what is best for their syndicated product. Many syndicators feel that Webcasting presents them with a controversial decision, up to and including the question of whether allowing local affiliates to broadcast on the Internet violates exclusivity agreements. It

IS TRADITIONAL RADIO DOOMED?

Today, Web radio's total audience is minuscule compared to the legions tuned to traditional radio. Not the phantom audience claimed by Hitmeisters in the industry, but the listenership that remains once the layers of hype are peeled away.

That's notwithstanding that Web radio has already reached a satisfactory technological level, with outstanding performance virtually around the corner. And with something like a quarter of the American population having suitable PC gear for reception.

Consumers Embrace Untethered Audio

To find an answer, let's look back at the evolution of radio. In radio's early decades, it had a monopoly on live mass home entertainment. Radios were bulky, expensive and tethered by a power cord, but people had no alternative so they accepted it. (Indeed, in some countries radio used to come into houses by wire, like cable TV.)

When television became a mass-market item after World War II, there was a brief period when console entertainment units were popular. Each of these jumbo jewels included a radio, record player and TV, and like early radio this do-it-all box was plugged into the wall.

But by the mid-fifties, radios, TVs and record players were increasingly being sold as separate units, albeit still tethered to wall sockets. With the popularization of the transistor a few years later, radios became completely portable, eventually leading to the development of the Sony Walkman. Transistors also made radio a universal and reliable feature of even the lowliest automobile.

Meanwhile, suburbanization has led to huge audiences for drive-time radio. Now, between this and the Walkman phenomenon, radio has overwhelmingly become a personal, mobile medium.

The history of the telephone has followed a similar pattern, with some delay. Wireless personal telephones are already to the point where wired phones are expected to become historical artifacts. It's hardly surprising, as cellular has allowed point-to-point audio (telephone) to possess the same mobility that consumers have flocked to for broadcast audio (radio).

With video, the story is different—it has succeeded as tethered, failed as mobile. Sony's first personal portable "Tum-Tum TV" goes back decades, but neither then nor since has handheld or mobile television been more than a novelty.

So, we have a long track record that shows us two things. First, consumers gravitate to mobile audio and resist tethered audio. Second, with TV and other video it has been exactly the contrary.

It is therefore hardly surprising that Web radio has languished in the shadows. To hear a simple radio station on the Internet calls not only for being tethered to a phone line and a power cord, but also to fire up a deskful of technological gear designed for on-screen and print video. So while Web radio makes engineering sense and has a certain novel appeal, it does not yet fit into the established pattern of human behavior.

Cellular Infrastructure = Web Radio Infrastructure

None of this is likely to last for long, as cellular and kindred technologies are creating the eventual infrastructure for *all* mobile communications. Indeed, in a precursor of Web radio via cellular, some radio stations are already transmitting over cellular/PCS networks.

But while a cellular/PCS provider might relay one or two local stations independent of the Web, once Internet reception via cellular becomes affordable and popular, station managers and listeners will be able to think about Web radio much differently. At that point, we would be able to get into the Star Trek stuff: Dick Tracy wristwatches . . . pliable cell receivers worn as shirt cuffs . . . glasses that double as A/V communications devices. Then the question would be, "Will established radio survive"?

While it may be tempting to write off traditional radio, chances are that it will continue to coexist comfortably with global Web radio precisely because FM and AM excel with local audiences and advertisers.

—*Lawrence Magne*

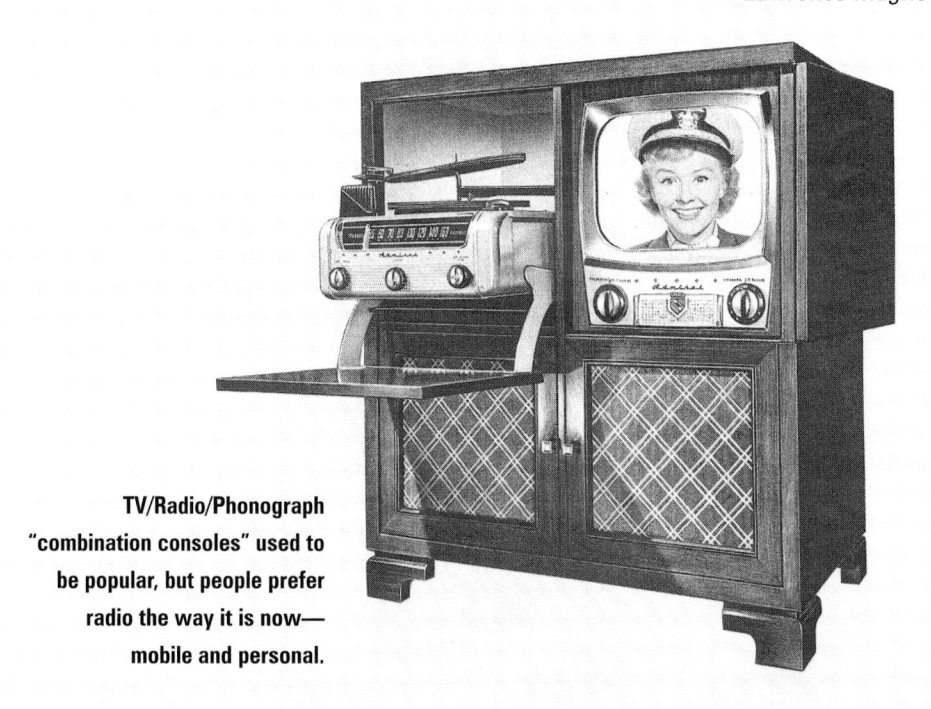

TV/Radio/Phonograph "combination consoles" used to be popular, but people prefer radio the way it is now— mobile and personal.

If you're looking to sample your competition in town and around the world, point your browser to Timecast.

appears that until significant studies can demonstrate that listeners—diary keepers—will list programs they've plucked from the Internet, many syndicators have elected not to allow their programs to be broadcast via the Web.

Better-Quality Local Reception

Web radio also attracts additional listeners locally because it puts in a high-quality signal to locations such as high-rise offices and condos where over-the-air signals are degraded. As modem speeds keep rising, CD quality Web radio should become commonplace within two or three years—even before over-the-air digital gets established in most markets within the United States.

Webcasting promoters often tout the fact that more and more companies are providing high-speed Internet access to their employees' desktops. Standard broadcast signals often cannot penetrate deep beyond the walls of large office complexes where employees would listen to the radio if they only could. Compared to the high-speed Internet connection offered to these employees, Webcasting uses a relatively small amount of bandwidth. This means that the employees can now listen to favorite local radio stations all day long, where before they couldn't listen at all.

It's also important to keep in mind that Internet users represent a demographically very desirable group. As I point out in my book, *CyberBuck$: Making Money Online*, the typical user has both an above-average education and an above-average income.

Multicasting Reduces Cost

One of the inherent problems with Webcasting is that a station's server can handle only a limited number of listeners. To get around this "unicasting" architecture, IP multicasting can be used. This allows Internet broadcasts to be delivered, like a regular radio broadcast, from one source—the station—to thousands of listeners' computers simultaneously without more than one server being used. It's effective and saves money for the broadcaster.

Stations getting into Webcasting need to check with their Internet service providers and Webcasting software firms for multicasting capabilities. RealNetworks' Real Broadcast Network (www.realnetworks.com) and broadcast.com (www.broadcast.com) each has specific software that allows broadcasting to be multicast. When a station signs up with, say, broadcast.com, the company provides a link from the station's normal Web page to its own "listen" page on the broadcast.com servers, from where the programing gets broadcast.

Is Webcasting Making Money?

Probably the most important question of all is: Are any radio stations actually turning Webcasting into a profit center?

The answer for the most part is no, but there are ways for stations to make money from their Websites (more in a moment). Webcasting can be viewed as an investment in the future or perhaps as something to be paid for from the promotional budget, but don't expect to generate any big bucks jumping into Webcasting now.

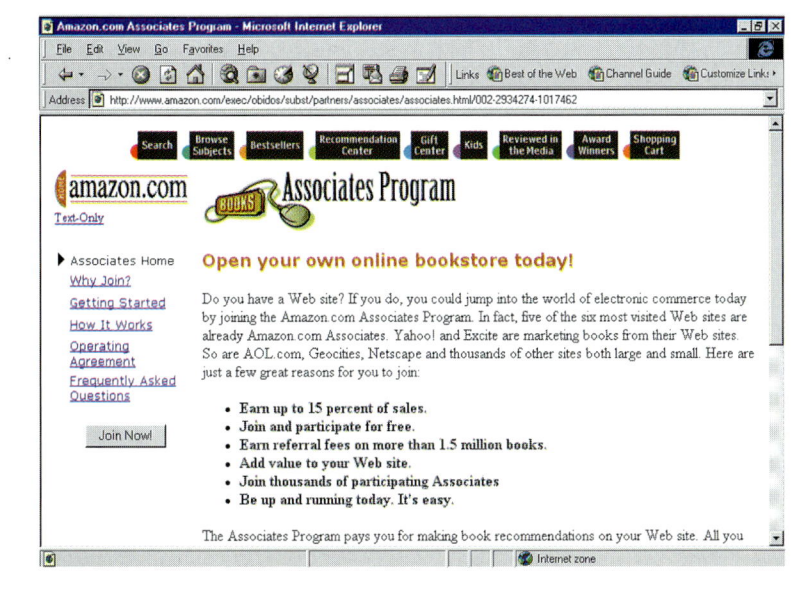

Striking deals with online bookstores and music resellers is one way to make money on the Web.

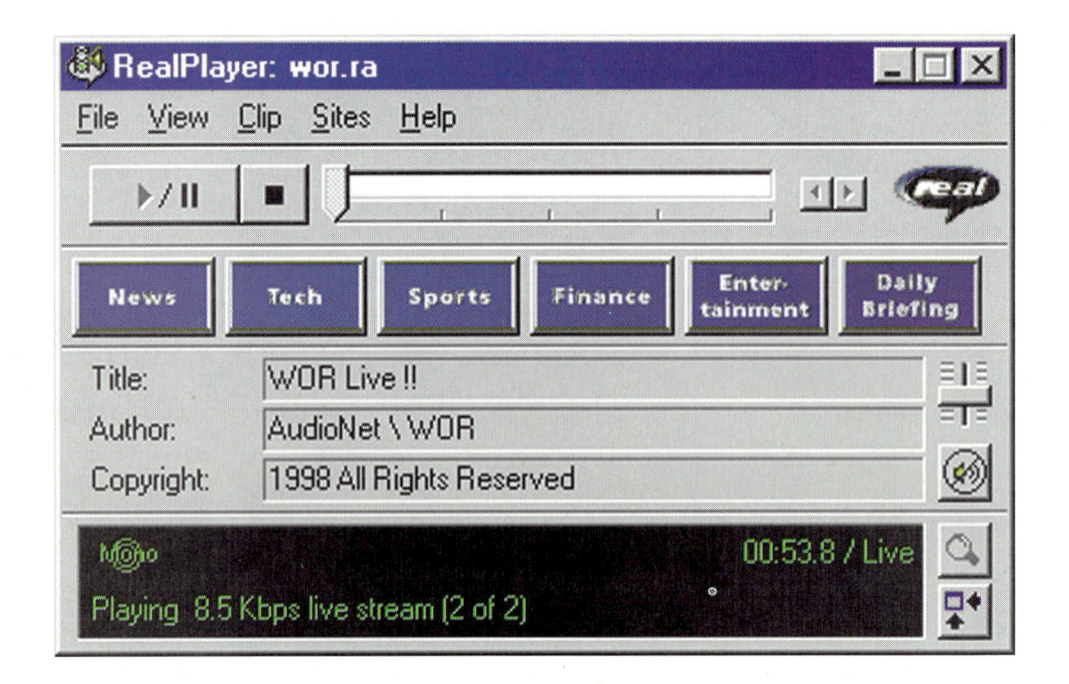

WOR Webcasts via broadcast.com, the world's largest Web radio network. Listeners are supposed to hear an audio commercial from broadcast.com before the station becomes audible, but some impatient listeners skip these by dragging the time pointer.

It appears that Webcasting may soon become more expensive. As far back as May 17, 1997, *Billboard Magazine* reported that the U.S. Copyright Office has been considering extending existing cable and satellite compulsory-licensing provisions to Webcasters. This means Webcasters would be subject to some sort of standard royalty payment for the right to Webcast music from local radio broadcasts.

Billboard also points out that the Recording Industry Association of America is proposing an alternative plan that would allow the music industry to decide what fees are paid by Webcasters. Whether the Copyright Office moves ahead with its current plans or the RIAA proposal is adopted, it's likely that some sort of increased royalties will soon be paid by music Webcasters.

How Stations Will Make Money

Most major metropolitan radio stations and syndicated programs now have some sort of presence on the Web. At the low end, there are the informational sites that provide photos of hosts, along with profiles, discussion topics and so forth. Somewhere in the middle, there are the sites that offer the photos and topics along with downloadable audio files of previously recorded on-air material. And at the high end are those stations and shows that have actually begun dabbling in interactive chats with station personalities or celebrities, as well as Webcasting.

But is this as far as the Internet/radio convergence can go?

In a word, no. I peeked into my cyber-crystal ball recently and what I saw in the future were all sorts of possibilities for new strategic alliances among book companies, consumer product manufacturers, news sources, stations and syndicated show hosts—alliances designed to bring information more effectively and efficiently to the masses (and of course make a few bucks doing so).

Book companies, for example, do a pretty good job of picking which authors will sell what topic. But every once in a while, that sleeper takes off and leaves the rest in the dust. Miscalculations like this cost companies money. Think of this. What if book companies could survey thousands of potential buyers ahead of time to assist in the decision-making process—at almost no cost? The Internet provides just such a mechanism.

That may sound fine for the book publisher, but why wouldn't the publisher just implement such a program through its own Website, and not a show or station site? The truth is, they could. But it would not be nearly as effective. The reason is that when someone wants to be entertained and informed on a myriad of topics, they turn on the radio, including talk radio.

In short, what I predict is an alliance of radio stations, shows and book publishers whereby books are prereleased in a survey format on radio Websites. Using existing Web software, survey results can be reported directly to the book publisher automatically, with no manual intervention on the part of the radio station.

Remuneration to the radio station can then be based on participation and/or the number of survey responses generated by the station's Website. And where can John and Jane Q. Public buy this book when it is released?

Technology exists that creates a unique opportunity for a radio station to expand its business into retailing by using its Website. The station could establish a formal alliance with a business that sells books online. Then the radio station could provide excerpts that will allow the listener to purchase that book from the allied e-business.

All this is now available. For example, Amazon Books, the world's largest online book retailer, already offers such a program for book purchases. A station can set up an online bookstore on its own site with direct links to Amazon. There's no inventory to carry and no orders to ship. If anyone purchases a book as a result of visiting that site, the Amazon system can tell, and the station automatically gets a cut from the sale. It wouldn't be difficult to adapt the same type of system to radio or show sites.

This can also be done with music, using CDnow and others. The catch is how can this be done without violating any official communications regulations. In order to avoid "payola" conflicts, stations may need to use paid programming time to promote their online radio business.

Innovative strategies like these have the potential to increase income from shows and boost earnings for stations. But in more general terms, they also have the ability to greatly increase the amount of traffic on a station's Website.

Web Advertising: Easy Money

This increased traffic is very important in itself, because any Website that can generate a substantial amount of traffic on a regular basis is a good candidate to sell advertising space. This is something a radio station or show should not overlook.

THE SLIPPERY SLOPE OF PIGLET RADIO

In the first edition of PASSPORT TO WEB RADIO, Freedom, California's commercial KPIG-FM got high marks for its freeform programming. With a fortysomething-plus audience, the station aired a Vietnam-era musical lifestyle no less valid than that, say, of the Big Bands around World War II.

Widespread Recognition Followed by Adjusted Format

A number of other organizations eventually also spotlighted KPIG for its distinctive format. Soon KPIG, the world's first commercial Web radio station, found it had almost as many online listeners as FM listeners—no surprise, given its hinterland location. But there were problems.

First, it used StreamWorks, and was about the last Web radio station to incorporate RealAudio. At typical modem speeds, StreamWorks just couldn't—and can't—begin to equal RealAudio for dependability.

Second, ads were scarce and usually local in nature. Clearly, advertisers were going for KPIG's modest FM signal, not its Web audience.

To get around this, KPIG finally installed RealAudio, and the difference is substantial. That's the good news.

"Aileen, the Traffic Queen" pigs out while giving weather and traffic information on KPIG.

The bad news is that the station's owners have shifted the format closer to that of a conventional rock station. No, you won't mistake KPIG for your local classic rocker, and it's still one of the best earfuls on the Web. Too, advertising, including for national accounts, is up. But the station is no longer compelling listening, the way it used to be.

Any Future for Diversity?

The question for the rest of us is whether KPIG has mismanaged its chance to be the leading light of Web narrowcasting, as cyber-prognosticator George Gilder's thesis about targeted advertising would suggest. Or is the station right, and the future of Web radio lies in something more closely approximating the homogeneous broadcast pattern found on local airwaves?

—Lawrence Magne. KPIG can be heard at www.kpig.com. George Gilder can be reached at gg@gilder.com.

KPIG's Dallas Dobro gets his morning fix huffing whipped cream. "Hold the Freon," says the environmentally conscious deejay.

Once traffic on a Website reaches a sustained, respectable level, the station should begin to explore the possibilities of offering online advertising—current broadcast advertisers may be prime candidates. The great thing about online advertising is that once it's in place, it costs virtually nothing to maintain. In short, if a station has the traffic to support the amount it is charging, it's easy money.

The broader audience brought by Webcasting allows stations to attract advertisers that normally might not be interested in reaching only a small, local market. But it's highly unlikely that Joe's Home Remodeling Service in the station's hometown really cares whether his spots are being aired worldwide on the Internet. Webcasting really doesn't do anything for businesses with no national or international appeal. This opens up the possibility of attracting Web-only ads for airing when local-interest spots are going out over the airwaves.

It is true that radio stations and syndicated programming are doing more with computers and the Internet than ever before, but it's really just the tip of the iceberg. In the next couple of years, the broadcast industry and the Internet will become so tightly integrated that consumers won't even think of them as two separate entities. The Internet will become a normal and expected part of the entertainment and information delivery business.

"Five Commandments" of Webcasting

Valerie Geller, president of Geller Media International and author of *Creating Great Radio*, may have put it best when she said, "Webcasting is great—provided that the show content meets the following criteria: 1) it's relevant, 2) it matters to the listeners, 3) the host cares about the material and can make the listeners care, 4) it tells the truth and 5) it isn't boring!" But that's true of any program on the air. In other words, Webcasting is a lot like traditional radio and, as such, requires ample talent, promotion and management.

And of course, a way to make money doing it.

_____

Kim Komando is the closest thing to a "Martha Stewart" among PC personalities. She is a successful TV host, Los Angeles Times *syndicated columnist,* WestStar TalkRadio Network *host,* Popular Mechanics *computer editor and best-selling author. Kim may be reached at komando@komando.com, or at the Website of the Komando Corporation at www.komando.com.*

Overleaf: Paris is the world's most visited city, and it has no less than 14 Webcasters. Two are in English, plus there's a fifteenth in the chichi Paris suburb of Neuilly. Not enough? There's also narrowcasting from the Sorbonne, which offers a variety of lecture courses in RealAudio from www.francelink.com/ radio_stations/sorbonne/ srfgrille.html. Digital Stock